READ THE WHOLE SERIES!

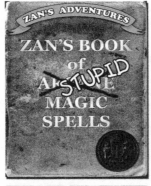

THE BARBARIAN MENDERCHUCK

Book 1 of the Menderchuck Saga

by

Paul Rodenburg

The characters and events portrayed in this book are fictitious. Any similarity to real persons, living or dead, is coincidental and not intended by the author.

No part of this book may be reproduced, or stored in a retrieval system, or transmitted in any form or by any means, electronic, mechanical, photocopying, recording, or otherwise, without express written permission of the publisher.

ISBN: 978-0-578-39972-0

If you purchased this book without a cover, you should be aware that this book maybe stolen property. If you did steal this book, then Menderchuck would be proud of you. Note: The author of this work does not condone stealing, unless it consists of downloading a car.

Dedicated to:

Fred & Betty

Thank you for all of

your love and support.

CHAPTER 1: THE BATTLE

Menderchuck the Terrible sat stoically upon his faithful steed, eyes focused upon the distant battle. In his line of work you didn't get the name "Terrible" by being bad at your job. He came from a long line of horse clan warlords. His father, and his father's mother before him, and his father's mother's father before that had all led clan Chuck; but none had been so swift, so aggressive, so successful as Menderchuck.

The Steppes of Rannsaka were his playground. Any merchant foolish enough to cross its vast prairies, soon became ripe pickings. Any village, that ignorantly failed to build a wall, was inevitably in flames as clan Chuck pillaged it. It was good times for those in the wall building business, but not much else. Even after all these years, Menderchuck was still amazed at the sheer number of villages that had failed to erect defensive fortifications.

If Menderchuck had spent some time peacefully strolling around these towns, he would have heard things like: "Putting up walls is locking ourselves in a cage. We're the victim there." "It's what the government wants you to do. See through the lies!" "If you want to build a wall by your house, fine, but leave my house out of it."

But what Menderchuck usually heard when he entered a town was more along the lines of: "Don't kill me!" "I told you inbreds that we should have built a wall!" "Don't kill me!" "Flee to the church!" "Ahhhh! He killed me!"

1

With a grim sigh, Menderchuck glanced up towards the great black vortex which swirled in the massive blue sky high above.

"Some days you eat the crow, some days the crow eats you," mumbled Menderchuck, remembering the sage advice of his long past grandmother.

While Menderchuck looked up, watching the multitude of carrion birds that flew in ominous swirling circles overhead, tens of thousands of beady greedy eyes gazed back down. Eagerly, the birds anticipated the coming feast. Though an immense flat ocean of grassland stretched to the horizon in all directions, the many hungry eyes of the flying vortex remained fixated upon a single sight. There, in the lee of a large lonely hill, two armies ferociously grappled with each other, locked in a desperate struggle between life and death.

"Archers!"

"Whaaat?" asked Menderchuck, glancing down from his horse towards the voice.

The urgent voice belonged to Pavel, Menderchuck's trusted bodyguard of many years. Loyally, the bodyguard stood beside his chief. Though Pavel was only five feet tall, he was built solid like an oak tree. Upon his body, he wore an old yak pelt that was fastened at the waist with a dirty rope belt. The pelt smelled as bad as it looked. Overly large worn leather boots encased his feet. A gleaming jeweled scabbard, which held a silver hilted saber, hung from his

2

modest rope belt. The plunder of some raid long past. In his left hand, he held the bridle of his horse who stood patiently beside him. In his right hand, tucked under his arm, he held a partially dented steel helmet that he had captured from a knight years ago.

"Duke Belloch's archers," anxiously repeated Pavel, pointing towards the hill. "They're taking the hill that overlooks our exposed right flank. If they take that..."

For a moment, Menderchuck silently glared at the distant hill. To the barbarian's dismay, Pavel was right. A host of enemy archers was rushing up the hill, quickly taking a position which overlooked his clan's unprotected right flank.

"Stupid Oleg!" rage fueled spittle erupted from Menderchuck's mouth as he spat out the words. "He was supposed to take the hill and protect the flank! I should have known better than to have listened to his plan! As father used to say, 'Plans are for cowards and swine. The only plan you need is a stout sword and someone to plunge it into. Now watch the door as I nap, son, and make sure your harpy of a mother doesn't come in here!'"

An awkward quietness overtook Pavel as he stood there holding his horse's reins.

"Your father said that a lot, did he?" curiously asked Pavel.

"Yes, all the time."

Menderchuck abruptly grabbed his horse's reins then looked down at Pavel.

"I'll take care of the archers. You, get the clan's flank turned," gruffly commanded Menderchuck.

"You can't take on the archers alone," desperately pleaded Pavel. "A man may have reverence for kings and queens, but arrows make no such distinctions."

"Fear not, I'll just ride so fast that they can't hit me," boldly exclaimed Menderchuck with a smile. "Now, old friend, follow your orders."

Defiantly, Pavel grabbed the bridle of Menderchuck's horse, holding it fast.

"Wear this," declared Pavel, knowing that it was useless to argue with his chieftain. "It's gotten me out of many a bad situation."

In one swift move, Pavel shoved his dented helmet up into Menderchuck's hands.

"What a dumpy, bent, dumb looking helmet," silently thought Menderchuck to himself, staring disdainfully at the helmet in his hands. "It's stupidly, stupid, stupid. How dare he ask me to wear this garbage?"

Menderchuck wasn't one for deep thoughts. Nonetheless, he smiled and put it on. Even the chief of clan Chuck knew that sometimes you wear stupid things for those you care about. And with that, he let out a mighty war cry. Urgently, he spurred his horse towards the endangered hill. There's a reason that he was known as Menderchuck the Terrible and not Menderchuck the Intelligent.

For a moment, Pavel's head hung low with a foreboding melancholy, watching the lone image of his friend riding hell bent across the plains straight towards the host of enemy archers. Then Pavel deftly mounted his own horse, speeding off to reinforce the clan's right flank.

It would be a lie to say that Menderchuck's horse thundered across the plains as it charged towards the archers' hill. The horses of clan Chuck had been bred for speed and stealth. It was little good if the enemy heard you and could close the gates before you arrived. And so, like the most heinous of farts, Menderchuck rode, quickly, silently, and deadly.

Menderchuck was halfway to the archer's hill, when that which would be his undoing would also become his salvation. In the midst of the vast host of archers upon the hill, a single archer noticed a glint to the south. It was the sun shining off of Pavel's helmet. The helmet that Menderchuck wore upon his very head.

The single archer pointed toward the lone distant rider that was charging them, crying out, "Barbarian!"

The host of archers turned their gaze from the nearby battle to the distant lone rider.

"OhhhhHHhhh," mocked one of the other

archers. "Is mommy's titty baby scared of a single barbarian?"

A hearty chuckle, at the lone archer's fear of a single man, spread through the archers' ranks like wild fire. As laughter erupted around him, Phebus, the archers' grizzled captain, stood there in stony silence. His veteran eyes remained transfixed upon the distant lone rider who was foolishly charging their hill.

"Menderchuck?" wondered Phebus aloud. "Who else would be so stupid as to charge a host of archers alone?"

But Phebus wasn't going to wait for an answer to his own question. He hadn't survived long enough to become an elder captain by waiting on his enemy. In a hurried instant, he turned his formation of archers southward.

"Ready, Aim, Fire," steadily commanded Phebus.

A volley of arrows erupted from the archers' bows, arching up into the sky in a cresting wave of death. Determinedly, Menderchuck watched the speeding arrows through the helmet's eye slits. Crouching down upon his horse, he spurred it on, faster and faster. *thud* *thud* *thud* Like a crashing wave, the arrows flew over speeding horse and rider, landing harmlessly in the ground behind them.

"Lower your aim. Fire!" brusquely commanded Phebus again as a hint of fear crept into his voice.

A second volley of arrows zipped up into the clear blue sky, arching for a moment, then zooming straight towards the earth. Deftly, Menderchuck maneuvered his horse, juking and snaking through the downpour of arrows which rained harmlessly around him. Man and horse moved as one, rapidly gaining on the archers' hill.

"It must be Menderchuck," whispered a worried Phebus to himself.

A few of the older wiser archers began to sneak towards the back of the assembled host.

"LOWER YOUR AIM, and FIREEEEE!" screamed out Phebus.

A third volley of arrows shot up into the clear blue sky. Once again, a wave of pointed death came crashing down towards the earth. Once again, Menderchuck tried desperately to ride through them, but this time one found purchase. A speeding iron arrow head shot square into Menderchuck's horse's head, killing it instantly in a spray of blood and brains. As the charging horse's legs gave way, the loyal steed crashed lifelessly to ground, skidding to a violent halt and leaving a trail of dirt behind it.

"AHHHH!!!" Menderchuck's yell reverberated loudly within the helmet.

His arms and legs flailed wildly as his body was abruptly catapulted from the dead horse, flying through the air like a rag doll. With a brutal clang, Menderchuck violently crashed helmet

7

first into a small boulder. Then his body collapsed limply to the ground, and the world went black.

CHAPTER 2: THE AFTERLIFE

Pain, it was the first thing that Menderchuck felt as he returned from the world of darkness. It radiated from his temples. It throbbed dully in the massive knot upon his head.

"Ugh, where am I?" grunted Menderchuck, forcing his eyes open and wincing at the light around him. "Is this the afterlife?"

His head swam as the blurry haze around him dissipated, revealing the humble interior of a small one room peasant hovel. The room's floor was made of hard packed dirt, and its walls were made of thick cut sod. In the center of the room, there stood a weathered table that leaned to the side as though it was literally on its last legs. On the room's far side, a handful of small animal pelts hung upon a rustic rack, drying in front of a weak crackling fire which burned in a rough misshapen stone fireplace.

"It don't look like the afterlife," mumbled Menderchuck, his nose reflexively scrunching up. "Ewwww, sure don't smell like the afterlife. Smells like some animal came in here to die."

Laying upon a crude straw covered wood bed that was just a bit too short for his feet, Menderchuck slowly turned onto his side with a grimace.

rattle *rattle* Menderchuck's startled heart raced as a rattling noise began to emanate from room's only door. Anxiously, his eyes lurched

9

towards the door, watching its handle turn.

Instinctively, Menderchuck's hand darted to the knife upon his waist, wrapping his fingers firmly around its white bone handle. Silently, with the steady hand of a seasoned warrior, Menderchuck pulled the blade from his belt. Then he rapidly laid back, hid the knife in the straw beside him, and closed his eyes in feigned rest. Alertly, his ears listened. First they heard the creaking of the opening door, then they heard the dull sounds of two pairs of footsteps entering the hovel.

"Look Harold," croaked the old peasant woman. "I don't care if the goat pooped on your feet first. That's no excuse for pooping on his. He's just a dumb animal, he doesn't know any better. You should."

The old woman took a couple steps towards the fireplace, then stopped dead in her tracks.

"Alright barbarian, get up," stated the old woman in a matronly voice. "I raised seven children. I can tell when someone is fake sleeping."

Sheepishly, Menderchuck opened his eyes and sat up in bed. He wasn't used to being called out in such a manner.

"And," continued the old woman. "You can put that knife away. You won't need it here."

Confused, Menderchuck returned his knife to his belt. Then he glanced up, quietly beholding the elderly peasant man and woman who stood before him.

"Hi, I'm Harold," declared the old man in friendly greeting. "And this is my wife Gretie. If ya want your, eh, helmet, it's under the bed."

Warily, Menderchuck leaned forward so that he could look beneath the bed upon which he sat. There he beheld the cold steely glint of Pavel's helmet. Gingerly, Menderchuck reached down with one hand, retrieving the helmet and lifting it up to examine. To his surprise, the helmet had a massive new dent from where it had hit the small boulder.

"Good thing you were wearing that," said Gretie as though talking to an old friend instead of a stranger.

"It's just not right," added the old man, shaking his head. "Ever since Duke Belloch invaded the Steppes, well, he's upsetting the natural order of things."

Menderchuck looked inquisitively at the old man.

"You lot," continued the old man, pointing at Menderchuck. "Beggin' ya pardon, but ya knew how to do it. Every year ya'd ride into our village hell bent on plunder. Kept us on our toes it did."

Gertie nodded in silent agreement as Harold ranted on.

"And ya'd come in, riding ya horses, screaming bloody murder and swinging all sorts of exotic weapons. It was a right proper show, it was. Sure, we was getting pillaged, but we got some bang for our buck. Does the boring old Duke Belloch do us proper like that? Of course not. He quietly marches in with his blue uniformed men. Each one looking the same as the next. How boring is that?"

A pregnant pause hung over the room as the old man waited for Menderchuck's reply.

"Ummm... very boring?" confusedly agreed Menderchuck.

"Exactly!" burst out the old man. "BORING! They ain't got no style or flair. But you barbarian horse riders, well I don't have to tell you, but every year around raiding time you'd be the talk of the town. Everyone trying to guess what hodgepodge of looted clothes, from far and wide, you'd all be wearing, no two the same."

"Remember," interrupted Gretie. "That year that barbarian man was wearing a lady's silk night gown."

Both peasants burst into a wheezy boisterous laughter as Menderchuck, who was at a loss for words, watched on.

"Ha! He thought he was all big and bad too!" laughingly gasped the old man. "Waving his sword about, bossing us all around, never realizing he was wearing lady's night garments. It took everything I could not to laugh in his face."

"It was too good," agreed Gretie, wiping a tear of

12

laughter from her face.

"See," resumed Harold, gesturing towards Menderchuck. "That's how you do it. Y'all brought us a proper dose of the world and some fine entertainment to boot. I mean sure, your men skewed my Uncle with spears, breaking his bones and piercing his muscle, staining his only shirt with rivers of blood, tearing the flesh from his body, popping his lungs so that they made this horrific blood bubbling.. guggghhllggg sound that will haunt my dreams until the day I die, BUT at least we knew where we stood and that's how we liked it. Uncle refused to reveal where his gold was, and got killed for it. It was a proper business transaction, it was."

Gretie nodded in quiet solidarity.

"The battle?" weakly asked Menderchuck, changing the subject.

"It's over," replied Gretie, solemnly shaking her grey head. "You lost from the looks of things. Days ago we were scavenging over the battlefield. Trying to find a nice sword for our grandson, Philli. He's almost five years old now. His whore of a mother..."

"Gretie!" exclaimed Harold. "That's our daughter."

"You know it's true. She's spent so much time on her back, it's a wonder she doesn't have permanent bedsores."

Harold shrugged his shoulders, unable to dispute

his wife's claim.

"So," continued Gretie. "His whore of a mother thinks he's too young for a real sword, but what does she know. Why my very kids played with swords much younger, and most of them never lost so much as a finger or an eye."

Menderchuck pictured a room full of children who looked like pirates. Or at least what he'd heard pirates looked like. He'd never actually met one before. In fact, he'd never even seen the sea.

"That's how we found you," finished Gretie. "So we brought you here to heal. That was days ago."

Menderchuck thought for a moment, then pulled his white bone handled knife from his belt, offering it handle first to the old woman.

"It is all I have to pay you for such kindness."

"Keep it barbarian," warmly smiled Gretie. "I have plenty of knives. Now, are you hungry?"

"I must return to my clan," replied Menderchuck, wobbling as he weakly attempted to stand.

Like a dark cloud drifting over the sun, a sad look crossed the old couples' faces.

"Eat first, gather your strength," compassionately commanded Gretie. "The dead aren't going anywhere."

CHAPTER 3: THE BATTLEFIELD

A cool stiff westerly breeze blew across Menderchuck's face, wiping away a fraction of the tears which flowed freely from his grieving eyes. Forlornly, as though he was the last living man in the Steppes, he stood upon the archer's deserted hill. Only days before, Duke Belloch's archers had stood in this very spot, raining death down on clan Chuck below.

Gretie and Harold had tried to warn Menderchuck that it would be bad, but nothing could have prepared him for what now lay before him. It seemed that the corpses of clan Chuck were spread across a square mile, interspersed with the corpses of the Duke's soldiers. Plump crows cawed loudly, greedily feasting upon the flesh of the dead.

Menderchuck wept for his slain warriors, but they had been more than just his warriors. They had been his life long friends and his family. He had already seen the decapitated head of his younger brother Mert and the lifeless bodies of numerous aunts, uncles, and cousins.

"I... I'm sorry," sullenly whispered Menderchuck from his guilt riddled soul. "I failed you all. If only I'd been faster, smarter... I'm sorry..."

Menderchuck's faltering words died in his mouth, choked off by his grief. When a loved one dies, so too dies a piece of your heart. And that day, Menderchuck's heart shattered like a dropped window pane.

For quite a time, the lone barbarian stood in quiet mourning upon the hill as the cool west wind poured over him. Then he turned southward. In the not too distant distance, he beheld the rock that he had collided with days before. Silently, he bent down, retrieving Pavel's dented helmet which rested at his feet. Then, helmet in hand, he set off down the hill and across the plains towards the boulder.

As Menderchuck approached the rock, he winced. For not far away, he spotted the lifeless body of his trusty steed. With a heavy sigh, he placed Pavel's helmet upon the large rock and then walked over to the horse's carcass. Grimly, he knelt besides the deceased mare, gently placing his hand upon its neck one last time.

"I'm sorry old friend," apologized Menderchuck.

After a few moments, Menderchuck rose to his feet, alone in the sea of grass. Then he began to wander in anxious circles, pushing the grass aside.

"Where is it? Where is it?"

His foot brushed against something hard. There, beside his feet, resting upon the hard ground, lay his war bow. The bow that his father had given him decades before, in a better time. Menderchuck lifted the bow from the ground and placed it upon his back before continuing his search.

"Where is it?! I must find it..."

The distant glint of the sun's warm rays reflecting off of cold steel caught his eye. Wasting no time, Menderchuck rushed to the spot, pushing the grass aside, and revealing that which he sought. There lay the sword of a thousand raids, his trusty blade, Arbjak. Solemnly, Menderchuck lifted the saber from the ground, gingerly wiping the dirt from it. After which, he placed the sword inside his belt.

"Why was I cursed to live?" Menderchuck forlornly asked himself. "What do I do now? Its all gone... Everything, washed away in a deluge of blood."

Standing upon the Steppes of Rannsaka, Menderchuck reached into his jerkin and pulled out an old letter. It was aged yellow and crinkled ever so slightly at the touch. Carefully, he opened it, studying its letters as he had a thousand times before. Though he could not read its words, he could recite them by heart. They had been read to him many times over the years. Gently, he placed a finger upon the signature at the letter's end.

"Maybe its finally time to take care of this," wistfully declared Menderchuck, refolding the letter and placing it back into his jerkin with care.

Then he turned his back to Pavel's dented helmet, which still rested upon the large rock behind him, and began to walk westward.

CHAPTER 4: OPPIDIUM

Far far away from the Steppes of Rannsaka, a lone raven silently glided through the cloudy sky. The bird gently tilted its wings and banked to the left. With a curious eye, it glanced down below toward the ancient city of Oppidium. Oppidium, a teeming walled metropolis, was the biggest city in the entire kingdom.

A large hill stood slightly off of the crowded city's center. Upon the hill, there stood the castle of the king. On paper, Oppidium was the king's seat of power, but his seat was seldom found within its walls. The illustrious monarch was often known to declare in his most stately voice, "I hate it, it smells of arse." Most people assumed that he was talking about the city. But in all truthfulness, the king's statement wasn't quite correct. The city smelled of a great many worse things as well.

A wide cobblestone road poured forth from the gates of the king's castle, slithered down through the town, and out of the city into the green country side beyond. This was the beginning of the king's highway or, perhaps, its end.

The city's streets zig and zagged like a drunken spider's web. Oppidium had never been properly planned. Like an unexpected child, it sorta just happened. As the city grew, people built up new houses outside of the crowded city's wall, and in time a new wall was built around them. Four times in total, as Oppidium grew over the centuries from a small backwater village into the capital of an entire kingdom.

18

A large river flowed through the heart of the city. The water that flowed into the city was clear and clean. The water that flowed out of the city was brown, full of trash, and often carried the bodies of those who went to "sleep with the fishes." (Not to be confused with Merfle the wizard, who romanced many a fish in an attempt to create his own race of mermen, with little success.)

High above the city, the raven circled once again. Then its little beady eyes found their target. Far below in the decaying market square, there sat a man upon a mighty stallion. The horse was large and black. Its bridle was made of gleaming brass that shone bright as day, and its leather saddle was adorned with precious stones.

Sitting astride the stallion was the Lord High Mayor of Oppidium. He wore a finely trimmed mustache upon his face and a funny triangle shaped golden hat upon his head. A red gown, with a giant white frilly cravat, adorned his body while white silk gloves covered his delicate hands. A thick golden chain, which held the crest of the city, was draped around his neck.

Pinned to his red gown were more than a dozen gold and silver medals that he, as Lord High Mayor, had awarded himself. The Order of Outstanding Service in the Event of a Stiff Breeze, the Commendation of Punctuality for always being on time to his own meetings (which really only officially started when he showed up anyway), the Merit of Bravery for the time he ran away from a suspicious looking street cat, bravely ran that is.

The Lord High Mayor had risen to prominence the old fashioned way. He inherited it. While the king was away, the Lord Mayor governed Oppidium, and the king was usually away. After slightly adjusting one of the multitude of medals which hung upon his person, the Lord Mayor looked up, surveying the market square around him, taking in its sights, its sounds, and its repugnant smells.

"Pre-owned fish, four for a tuppence!" shouted out a fish monger.

The reek of rotten fish drifted throughout the square, emanating from the pile of half eaten fish which covered the fish monger's market stall. If someone hadn't known better, they may have thought that the fish monger had spent the better part of last night fishing the rotten fish out of other people's trash to resell. If someone had known better, than they would have known that that was exactly what the fish monger had done. Recently he had heard of the arcane magic called "marketing" and was giving it a go to tremendous results.

"Soggy vegetables! Get your soggy vegetables here!" exclaimed another merchant who jealously watched the vast line of people queuing up to buy pre-owned fish.

A few rabid dogs ran carelessly between the vibrant stalls of the busy market square. While several other dogs, who were too poor to afford rabies, watched on with envy.

A group of five year old children played tag in a

corner of the market. Their joyful squeals filled the air as they ran about. The Lord High Mayor looked at the children and frowned.

"Children are the future," thought the Lord Mayor. "And, that is a problem. Children grow up to be adults, and adults are problematic. They constantly bother me with whiney pleas to fix their problems, or worse, cause problems themselves. Everyone that was ever bad, was once a child. It is best to just try to and nip it all in the bud."

He had tried to deal with the problems of children. He had offered an all expenses paid birth control program for the city. Any pregnant woman could be thrown off of the highest battlements of the king's castle to plunge to their deaths on the cobblestone below at no cost to themselves. What a deal! But no one had accepted the offer.

He had thought that, perhaps, if he led by example, then the birth control program might succeed. The Lord Mayor had tried to convince his own pregnant wife to throw herself from the battlements as a show of goodwill to the program; but she had stubbornly, selfishly refused.

"Women," he thought, "are so difficult."

His thought was interrupted by a woman in the market square before him. She was a kindly looking elderly woman in a black dress who was carrying a black purse. Slowly, she walked towards the group of energetically playing five year olds. As she neared the children, she opened her bag.

"Who wants candy?" she asked with a kindhearted smile.

Like moths to a flame, the young children ran over to the old woman. Gingerly, she pulled pieces of candy from her purse and handed them one by one to each child.

"Are you lovelies having a fun day?" inquired the old woman. "When I was your age, I too loved to play tag with my friends. They're all dead now."

"More candy!" grunted a child who had already eaten his piece.

"I'm sorry hunny, but that's all I have."

"More! More candy!" cried the children.

The old lady chuckled, "Dears, next time I come to market I'll bring you all some more, my you are full of energy."

"LIAR!" screamed out one of the wee children, pointing an accusatory finger at the old woman. "Stop holdin' out on us, ya old hag!"

While the poor old lady stood there confused; a small child, with a steely gaze in his eyes, hauled back and punched the old lady in her baby maker.

"Ouuufff!" gasped the old woman, bending forward in pain as her wooden dentures shot out of her mouth and flew into the mud before her.

"Make with da candy, ya old broad!" demanded the five year old.

As the gang of wee children began to advance menacingly upon the old lady, she desperately clenched her purse handle, swinging it in a mighty arc. With the speed and dexterity of youth, several children leapt backwards avoiding the swinging purse, but the child who had punched her was not so lucky. The purse smashed him square in the face, knocking him butt first into the mud. There he landed with a mighty thud.

For a moment, a look of shock and surprise overtook the boy's face, as though he was trying to figure out how to respond. Then, after a moment of contemplation, he knew the appropriate response. Loudly, he began to cry while looking around to make sure that other people noticed.

The old lady knew that this was her one and only chance to escape. As the wee child cried in the mud puddle before her, the old woman grabbed the hem of her skirt and began to run.

"Eat my buttocks, you street demons!" she yelled out, running past the gang of tiny street urchins.

Needless to say, this angered the gang of children who began picking up horse dung from the street, pelting her fleeing body with it.

"Hmmmm," thought the Lord Mayor to himself

as he watched the old lady run for her life. "Good for her. I would have bet on the child gang myself. I guess you learn something new everyday."

Child related violence was sadly on the rise in the city. Why just last week a roving mob of toddlers had taken over the Oppidium art museum. They had defaced priceless works of art with jam smeared hand prints and crayon scribbles. By the time the city guard had arrived to put down the disturbance, the first floor of the museum was completely ruined. The guards would walk in to find a floor sticky with fruit juice and covered with tuckered out toddlers who were napping. Thank god for naptime, it may have been the only thing that saved the museum's second floor. These things troubled the Lord Mayor.

"Why are these children such lazy good for nothings?" condescendingly wondered the mayor. "They need to pull themselves up by their tiny bootstraps, as I had. Why, by the time I was their age, I had already sacked my first nanny."

Sacking in Oppidium consisted of putting an employee in a sack and beating them with a reed until they became silent. The Lord Mayor couldn't quite remember why he had sacked his nanny as a child. Vague lingering memories alluded to a contested bedtime struggle. Whatever the reason, the sacking had been his idea, and thus he was confident that it had been the correct action.

This whole time, the raven, who'd been circling high above the city of Oppidium, had been slowly descending. The black bird glided silently into the market square, landing gently onto the Lord High Mayor's shoulder. Unfazed, the mayor sat there upon his mighty steed while the raven leaned forward, whispering into his ear.

"What happened?" asked the mayor. "Big battle on the Steppes? hmmm? Clan Chuck all dead? Interesting... Rather tasty corpses?"

With the last whisper, the Lord Mayor looked suspiciously sidelong at the raven, thinking "scavenger birds are odd creatures." Then he reached into his red gown and pulled out a large cracker. With large greedy eyes, the raven stared at it in eager anticipation. Suddenly, the Lord Mayor tossed the cracker into the air. Like an arrow escaping a taught bow, the raven shot off of the mayor's shoulder, grabbing the cracker in mid-air and then flying away.

"Finally," thought the Lord Mayor, "some good news."

Over the years, he had surely meant to make a modicum of effort to ensure that the boy had survived.

"What was his name? Turdleson? Sigh... who can even remember these peasants and their stupid names?"

But in reality, he had forgotten about the boy and the potential threat that he had posed over a decade ago.

"I guess it doesn't matter now," proudly boasted

the Lord Mayor, spurring his horse forward through the bustling market square. "One more potential problem crossed off of my list. Sometimes the best action is no action. Well done me."

CHAPTER 5: TORFULSON

"AwwHHHH," yawned Torfulson, rubbing the sleep from his eyes as his footsteps crunched on the gravel road below.

For a moment, he paused and looked back towards the city of Oppidium. There he saw a large raven fly up out of the city, disappearing into the sky above.

"Birds of a feather," smiled Torfulson, feeling a kindred spirit.

Each day he too left the crowded confined walls of the city, escaping to the freedom of the country on his way to his job as a milkmaid. He hadn't wanted to become a milkmaid, but it was the only job that he could find.

"Well, best not be late," quietly declared Torfulson, a skinny young man of above average height with short cut black hair.

Then he hoisted his bag high onto his shoulder and turned away from the city. The gravel road crunched under his feet once more as he resumed his journey toward the dairy farm.

CHAPTER 6: THE DAIRY FARM

Unfortunately for many an unwary traveler, the stench of farmer Jennix's immense dairy farm could be smelled long before the estate came into view. Situated off of a busy dirt road that lay only an hour by cart from Oppidium, the farm filled a wide open plain that was nestled between several green rolling hills and an ancient forest.

The forest was a wash with gangs of half wild pigs who roamed mercilessly in search of forage. Come harvest time, the local peasant farmers would brave the forest, repeating their yearly ritual of rounding up the pigs, recovering those which were their own, arguing over the parentage of new pigs, then deciding which pigs were meant for slaughter and which would be housed in their pigsties for next year. Though the fertile forest of pig forage lay just outside of the boundary of Jennix's farm, he refused to lower himself to such a ritual, for cows were his business.

To the residents of distant Oppidium, the name "Jennix" stood for above average quality dairy products. And it was that city's massive dairy demand that had made Jennix a rich man. For his employees, the name "Jennix" stood for an abrasive micromanager with a short temper. And for the local peasant dairy farmers, the name "Jennix" stood for a greedy man who owned more than enough pasture land yet still unleashed his massive herds upon the communal grazing land, picking them clean.

Each morning, milkmaids from far and wide made their pilgrimage down the dusty dirt road, turning southward onto dairy farm's long driveway. As they approached the estate proper, their eyes beheld a farm of unparalleled size. To the far south, immense pens, flanked on both sides by large barns, held massive herds of cattle that dwarfed the populations of most large cities. North of the pens, there stood a gaudy two story stone manor of relatively recent build. It was, in no uncertain terms, a farmer's idea of what a regal manor lord's house should look like.

To the west of the manor, there stood a row of long ranch houses that housed the ranch hands who lived on site. To the east of the manor, there stood a barn which doubled as a workshop and distribution center. Each day, a multitude of carts arrived to it. Some of the carts were large and clean. These tended to carry the farm's dairy products far and wide for sale. Some of the carts were small and filthy, carrying away the farm's immense excess of cattle droppings to sell to local farmers for fertilizer.

And in the midst of this bustling farm, dominating the surrounding buildings, there stood farmer Jennix's great open air barn. A wooden feat of exceptional engineering, the barn had no walls. Instead, a considerable multitude of thick wooden posts, that had been cut long ago from the nearby forest, held up barn's great roof. And great was the roof indeed for below its immense protection an army of milkmaids could milk entire herds at a time come rain or come shine.

"It's the largest barn in the whole kingdom. Get on my barn level, losers!" farmer Jennix was often found bragging to others.

While the droning buzz of flies and the rancid wafting smells of cow dung filled the dairy barn's wall-less rooms, a multitude of milkmaids sat upon small wooden stools, hunched partially beneath cows, diligently milk, milk, milking away. As cows were milked dry, ranch hands led them away, leading in new cows for milking. And in the same way, as wooden buckets filled with milk, ranch hands carried them from the barn to the waiting carts. Thus the milkmaids could be ever milking without ever having to leave their appointed work stools.

And so farmer Jennix's massive open air barn was filled with the noisy commotion of the great host of his briskly bustling workers who were all busily focused on their appointed tasks. Well... all, except one.

In the midst of the commotion, near the center of the barn, sat Torfulson the reluctant milkmaid. He sat upon a small stool, hunched beneath the farm's most impressive cow, Mrs. O'Leary. Mrs. O'Leary was farmer Jennix's prized dairy cow. She stood a head taller than the rest of the herd, and her udders were almost twice as large. Torfulson knew in his heart that she was the perfect subject for his secret experiment. He had even gone so far as to arrive an hour early to work today, just to snag the chance to milk Mrs. O'Leary.

"Moooo," lowed Mrs. O'Leary as Torfulson tried

once again to attach a hose to the cow's teat.

"There there, old girl," reassured Torfulson, gently patting the cow on her side. "This won't hurt one bit, in fact it'll make your life a whole lot easier."

Sweat dripped down Torfulson's brow as he tried once again to attach his secret contraption to the cow.

"In fact," explained Torfulson to the cow. "It'll make all of our lives easier, and, I hope, it'll make me wealthy. No more living payday to payday. No more fear of rent going up. No more fear of losing my home. No more having to choose between food or a doctor in time of illness. Oh, and I'll be able to buy some shoes. Not just shoes, but new shoes! Maybe those fancy kinds, with the brass buckles."

pop Torfulson attached one of his contraption's hoses onto the cow's teat, then he tugged it gently, confirming that it was secure.

"Moooo."

"Look I get it," comforted Torfulson. "New things can be scary, but in reality its not that complicated. It's just a device to milk cows, only a lot faster. The four hoses on this end, they connect to four of your teats. The hose on the opposite side, I suck on that, and then all four teats get milked at once. It'll make milking four times faster, which will greatly increase profits. At least I believe it will... this is my prototype."

pop Torfulson connected another hose to another of the cow's teats while Mr's. O'Leary stood there blankly chewing her cud.

"Once I can prove it works. I'm sure farmer Jennix will make me his partner. And if he doesn't, well someone will want this. It could make any dairy farmer rich."

pop Torfulson connected a third hose to a third teat. Unbeknownst to him, his secret work had not gone unnoticed. Summoned by their curiosity, a small group of milkmaids and ranch hands had begun to assemble around him, silently watching his work.

pop Torfulson attached the fourth hose to a fourth teat. With a relieved sigh, he sat up straight upon the stool and wiped the ample sweat from his face. Then he grabbed the lone hose, which emerged from the contraption's other side, and lifted it to his face.

"Goodbye hard work, hello easy sucking," declared Torfulson out loud to himself.

"That's what your mom said," replied the milkmaid Clara to uproarious laughter behind him.

Furiously, Torfulson spun around, glaring at Clara. If looks could kill, she would have died on the spot. Torfulson's steely gaze sent a shiver through the milkmaid.

"I.. I'm sorry..." mumbled Clara in embarrassed apology as the ranch hands around her still roared with laughter.

With a grunt and a furrowed brow, Torfulson slowly turned on his stool back towards the cow. Once again, he reached down and grabbed the milking contraption's free hose. Once again, he lifted it to his face. Then he placed it into his mouth and began to suck, but nothing happened.

"You're definitely are an expert at sucking," teased a ranch hand.

Torfulson rolled his eyes, paused to let out a deep breath, then sucked even harder on the hose. His eyes bulged slightly and his veins popped, but no matter how hard he sucked, nothing happened, not even a single drop of milk. Torfulson wheezed, taking a moment to catch his breath. As he did, he noticed a ranch hand in the assembled crowd give him a slow wink.

"Weird," thought Torfulson.

Undeterred by his failure thus far, Torfulson took in a massive breath and then forced it out. He grabbed the lose hose of the contraption, shoved it back into his mouth, and sucked harder than he had ever sucked before. He sucked until his cheeks turned red. He sucked until the veins in his neck began to bulge. He sucked until he saw little stars orbiting around him. He sucked until the laughter around him became muffled and distant in his ears. He sucked until the world went black, and he collapsed into a nearby pile of fresh cow manure. At least it was a soft warm landing.

"Wake up ya lazy git!" screamed out a familiarly angry voice though the haze. "I don't pay you to sleep!"

"Man, whoever Jennix is laying into sounds like they are in a world of trouble," thought Torfulson with a dopey smile as he lay in a world of stinky warm blackness.

Slowly, Torfulson blinked his eyes, dispelling the darkness and revealing a furious farmer Jennix, who stood over him glaring downward.

"Oh, cow poopy."

The words had slipped out of Torfulson's mouth before he could even think.

"And that's another thing!" screamed the irate farmer Jennix. "Ya made a mess of my perfectly good cow manure. Ya muck it, and we spread it. Ya don' wear it! Dumb fool, thinking you can suck the milk outta a cow with hoses. Sucking a cow's teat is a calf's job! You seem to have the brain of a calf, ya half wit!"

More than a few of the assembled milkmaids and ranch hands laughed at Jennix's insult which brought a cruel prideful smile to the furious farmer's face. Then, in one swift move, farmer Jennix reached down, roughly pulled the milking contraption from his cow, and slammed it angrily to the ground. As the contraption collided with the ground, it broke apart into a half dozen pieces.

"Now!" commanded Jennix. "Get your dumb

arse up, and get back to milking. With your hands this time, as the gods intended. And keep your foul contraptions away from my beasts!"

Embarrassed, humiliated, and covered in cow droppings, Torfulson obediently crawled up to his knees and sat once again upon the small wooden stool. Silently, he grabbed a nearby pail, placing it beneath the cow. Carefully, he wiped the cow dung from his hands and onto his pant legs until they were reasonably clean. Then he began to milk the cow by hand.

"Mr. Jennix!" came the shout of a ranch hand from beyond the barn. "Mr. Henderson is here to see you about stud fees."

"I'm coming, Todd," shouted out the farmer in reply.

Out the corner of his eye, Torfulson watched farmer Jennix walk away. As soon as the farmer was out of sight, Torfulson reached down, carefully grabbing the pieces of his broken contraption, and stowing them beneath his stool for safe keeping. Then he reluctantly returned to milking Mr's. O'Leary by hand.

CHAPTER 7:
THE JOURNEY HOME

As dusk's tinted sky began to descend upon the earth, Torfulson began his long retreat home in manure covered clothes. A host of hungry flies and gnats, drawn by the smell, accompanied him. The occasional traveler, which he met on the long and winding dirt road, made sure to steer a wide berth around him.

The evening grew long as Torfulson finally approached the walled city of Oppidium. A kindly guard smiled and waved for a brief moment. The guard's nose scrunched in revulsion, and his smile morphed into a grimace as Torfulson walked past through Oppidium's front gate.

Torfulson traveled down the King's Highway into the city while the crowds before him made way like a ship cutting through the sea. Without looking, he could feel their judging eyes upon him. He could hear people coughing around him at the revolting smells which rolled off of his clothes. He sighed with relief when he finally came to his exit. Hurriedly, he turned off of the King's Highway, heading down a side street towards his home in the slums.

Torfulson navigated the narrow crooked back streets of the slums with veteran precision. He had grown up on these very streets and knew them well. Soon his journey ended outside of a small dilapidated wood shack. He stopped and looked up at the shack. To most people it would have been a pitiful hovel, but to him it was the only home that he had ever known. Unceremoniously, he tossed his bag upon the shack's front stairs and then looked down at his filthy clothes.

"No way I'm polluting the house with these poo poo rags," sighed Torfulson to himself. "I gotta clean up, before I go in."

His eyes began to scan the ramshackled neighborhood around him for a solution. Soon they landed upon an old horse trough which lay across the street.

"It'll have to do."

Determinedly, Torfulson strolled across the dirt street to the old horse trough. Once there, he hastily removed his soiled clothes, stripping down to his underwear. Then he dropped his dirty clothes down into the cloudy horse water below with a splash.

"Ugh..." grunted Torfulson, slowly bending down to his knees beside the horse trough.

Diligently, he tried to make the best of a bad situation, scrubbing his filthy clothes in the slightly less filthy water.

"PERVERT!" screamed out a woman behind him.

Wide eye, a suddenly startled Torfulson turned and beheld a woman who stood in the street pointing right at him.

"Jim! There's a nude pervert in the street, and he wants to touch me!" yelled out the woman.

Torfulson sat perfectly still, like a spooked deer. His eyes grew larger and larger as he saw a large muscular man come around the corner.

"Please don't be Jim.." whispered Torfulson pleadingly to himself.

The large muscular man and the woman rapidly advanced on Torfulson.

"Jim, that's him!" screeched the woman pointing at Torfulson. "PERVERT!"

"What do you think you're doing here, creep?" demanded Jim in a deep booming voice.

Torfulson looked up nervously at Jim. Jim was at least a foot taller than him and probably a hundred pounds heavier.

"Ummm," nervously gulped Torfulson, slowly rising to his feet. "I'm washing my clothes in the horse trough. I fell in cow poopy today."

"PERVERT! He wants to touch me right now. I can see it in his eyes!" screeched the woman again.

"This is a perfectly good neighborhood," bellowed Jim, who was apparently too new to the neighborhood to know that his statement was untrue. "We can't have nude creeps like you trying to touch up our woman folk! I oughtta pound the pervert out of you!"

"Do it Jim, beat him til he bleeds his own pervo blood all over himself," the woman egged on.

"No, no, no, I'd never want to touch your wife," pleaded Torfulson.

"Why?" asked the man angrily. "Are you saying she's ugly?! Are you saying I married a hideous she-beast, and I should have listen to my mother and married that sweet girl from down the block instead?"

Torfulson stood there silently, very very confused. Both man and woman glared at him expecting an answer.

"Maybe?" replied Torfulson, shrugging his shoulder noncommittally.

It was the wrong answer. The woman sucker punched Torfulson hard in the gut. He collapsed backwards and landed in the horse trough behind him with a splash. Then the woman began shouting at Jim.

"Hideous she-beast?!?! You and your mother can go sleep on the streets for all I care!"

"Gladice!" Jim bellowed back. "I am not in the mood for your crap today!"

The couple angrily turned their backs to Torfulson and stormed off, shouting at each other the whole way. Once the couple was out of sight, Torfulson slowly pulled himself out of the horse trough.

"Well," Torfulson weakly tried to comfort himself as the dirty horse water dripped off of his drenched body. "I guess that takes care of the bath I needed..."

Defeatedly, Torfulson scooped up his wet clothes and walked back across the street to his decrepit shack. There he opened his discarded bag and pulled out an iron key. Key in hand, he unlocked the shack's old wooden door. It swung open with a small lonely creak, revealing the main room of his two room shack. Before him stood an empty table beside a dead fireplace. Torfulson then stepped into the room's lonesome silence and closed the door behind him.

CHAPTER 8: 3 A.M.

clack *clack* Came the noise of the outhouse's door through Torfulson's open bedroom window. Torfulson smiled faintly at the old familiar sound. Most people would have been less than thrilled to have a neighborhood outhouse right outside of their bedroom, but for Torfulson it was the comforting sounds of home. Torfulson chuckled lightly to himself as a distant childhood memory flickered to life in his brain.

"I remember all the hours I used to people watch out of that window, until Mom told me I had to quit. Mrs. Watterson had complained to Mom. She said it was disturbing to take a poo, then emerge from the outhouse to see me staring at her with unflinching eye contact. Ha, I must have looked like some creepy child."

Torfulson's words bounced off of his tiny bedroom walls. There he lay on his back, surrounded by darkness, upon a modest bed that was a bit too short for his feet. With a light grunt, he rolled over to his side. His eyes gazed out through his bedroom window to the half moon which hung in the cloudless night sky.

Since he had arrived home hours earlier, Torfulson had done his best to put his embarrassing milking contraption failure out of his mind, but with little success. Finally, at this late hour, his mind relented. Instead, his brain dusted off the tried and true 3 a.m. failure reel, and began to play it in the theater of his mind.

His first and last date, where he had trusted a fart that he shouldn't have.

"Sigh... that wasn't even the worst part of the night."

The time a waitress had placed his birthday dinner before him and said, "enjoy your meal."

"You too," he had replied as embarrassment had instantly washed over him.

That was the magic of the 3 a.m. failure reel. It stored not only your memories of failure, but also your feelings of guilt, embarrassment, and shame which accompanied such recollections. During the day, no one would wish to visit a theater that showed such things. But at 3 a.m. the mind's theater was the only open theater in town, whether you liked it or not.

For a moment, Torfulson smiled at the next scene that played before him. In his mind's eye, he was eight years old again. Eagerly he watched his neighbor, old man Karl, carving majestic life like creatures using only a carving knife and a block of wood.

"They looked like they could come to life at any moment," reminiscenced Torfulson. "A tiny army of bears, unicorns, brave knights, and scary dragons. I'd wanted nothing more than to make and have my own. Huh, I remember even hoping I could carve and sell some, to help Mom with the overwhelming bills. I just needed to get the money to buy a carving knife."

Torfulson's smile faded while the next scene began to play, for he had seen this reel many times before. His eight year old self had rushed around the neighborhood for months, taking any spare jobs that he could find. Feeding Mrs. Watterson's cat "Bitey." His fingers had attested to the accuracy of the cat's name. Holding the torch for Mr. Ramone as he did late night cart repairs. Young Torfulson had been amazed to learn how many wrong ways one can hold a torch. It had been a much tougher job than he had anticipated. He had even taken the disgusting job of cleaning out the neighborhood outhouse. The horrors of which are better left to history.

"I remember finding the perfect piece of carving wood, in the alley behind the Watterson's home. I brought it home and hid it under by bed. Each night, I'd check to make sure it was still there, just waiting til I had a knife to carve something amazing out of it. But not just something, it was going to be Argoth the Cruel."

Argoth the Cruel was a wolf, but not just any wolf. He was the first of his pack and the most feared wolf in the Eastwoods. At least, so the legends told. Each night, eight year old Torfulson had studied his perfect piece of carving wood, trying to see the wolf in the wood. He studied its grain, studied its curves, visualizing the moment when a miniature wooden Argoth the Cruel would emerge.

"And then the day came. I collected all my hard earned pennies, carefully counting them one by one. When I was assured I had enough, I rushed to Bobbert's."

Bobbert's Pawn Shop seemed like a wonderland of amazement and variety to an eight year old. Wedding rings, lanterns, dented swords, partially charred armor, it seemed as though the pawn shop had some of everything. It hadn't taken young Torfulson long to find the object of his desire. Behind a glass case, surrounded by daggers, there lay a carving knife. Sure, its blade had a nick or two, and its wooden handle was worn; but to Torfulson it had shined with eternal promise.

"I bought it in an instant, then walked home. I wanted to run home, but I remember walking slowly because mother had always told me to never run with knives," chuckled Torfulson to himself. "Bobbert put it in a box, I could ran all I wanted. Funny how we are as kids."

The light of the mind's theater dipped for a moment, as the scene cut to eight year old Torfulson sitting on the front steps of his home, carving knife in one hand, wood in the other, diligently shaving off bits of wood.

"I spent hours working on it each night," remembered Torfulson. "Whittling the wood, and sometimes bits of my fingers on accident. Oh well, what is a little blood when making art. The gods of art demand such sacrifices. And then, one day, it was finished. I had done it, made my own little Argoth the Cruel out of wood. I was so proud that I excitedly rushed to my mother. I had to show her."

44

Wood figurine in hand, he had run into his home. There, in their shack's main room, he found his mother and this month's "Uncle."

"Mummy, look what I made!" young Torfulson had exclaimed as he had handed the carving to his mother.

Gingerly, she took the wooden miniature from young Torfulson. Carefully, she studied the little wooden wolf.

"It's Argoth the Cruel. I made it!" triumphantly declared young Torfulson.

"It looks like a crap I took this morning," taunted this week's 'Uncle.' "More like Argoth the poo."

The man laughed heartily at his own joke while Torfulson's mom gave the man a dirty look. Then she gently handed the wooded miniature back to Torfulson and put a reassuring hand upon his shoulder.

"I think you did an excellent job, hunny. I look forward to seeing what else you make. Now run along outside and play. I need to have a word with Carl, here."

With slunk shoulders and a downcast head, eight year old Torfulson dejectedly wandered out from the house into the street beyond. It was then that the sounds of his mother's shouting erupted from the shack behind him.

"If you ever talk to my son like that again, I'll rip off your dick and force feed it to you!"

But Torfulson had not heard a word of it. His eyes were transfixed upon the wood miniature in his hand.

"What was I thinking?" the young boy had lamented, holding back tears. "This looks nothing like Argoth. It's horrible, awful. I could never carve as well as old Karl. Why did I even try?"

Pride had given way to the overwhelming feelings of futile failure. As he stared at the wooden miniature, anger and frustration had filled his soul.

"I hate you. You're disgusting. I never should have made you. I wish you never existed. I never want to see you again!"

Young Torfulson reached back with a blind fury, throwing the wooden wolf as hard as he could. The wooden miniature tumbled and spun as it flew through the air. Suddenly young Torfulson's fury turned to horror as the miniature arched downward, smashing into the neighbor's window with a glass shattering crash.

"OWWWW!" shouted out old Karl from inside the house. "Who the hell threw this hard piece of poo at me?!!?"

Crying, young Torfulson had turned away and ran. Never again would he attempt to carve. The mind's theater began to go dark as this particular 3 a.m. reel reached its end.

"Thanks a lot, brain," sarcastically mumbled

46

Torfulson as he drifted off to sleep.

CHAPTER 9:
THE MILKING MACHINE

The months passed, as they tend to do. The failed milking contraption lay untouched in a dark corner of Torfulson's hovel, gathering dust. Occasionally, while eating a hurried breakfast before work, Torfulson would glance over at his failed machine.

He had wracked his brain to no avail in an attempt to discover how to make the contraption work. If Torfulson had been well educated, he might have realized that what he needed to do was to significantly increase the pressure differential in the milking contraption, but he was not well educated.

Instead he figured, "The problem is that I don't suck enough. I need to suck more. More than anyone has ever sucked before!"

He had gotten an odd look from Mrs. Watterson, who had overheard his ranting as she had walked past his open window. But that was then. Today he was focused on a much different quest.

The sights and sounds of a multitude of shoppers filled Oppidium's bustling market district. The delicious smells of fried foods wafted between the many colorful market stalls which lined the square. It was best not to inquire what the fried food was made of, but better to just enjoy its crispy and intriguing tastes. The savory smells teased and tempted Torfulson's nose. His mouth watered as he passed "Earl's Deep Fried

Everything." Earl had built a reputation on being willing to batter, slather, and deep fry anything.

Torfulson was already long past when Earl slipped and dropped the crate that he was carrying. It crashed to the ground, smashing open. A host of frogs leapt from the demolished crate in every direction. Helplessly, Earl chased after a few in vain, but it was too late. The majority of the frogs had already escaped into the bustling crowd.

Hungrily, Torfulson snuck a glance at a bright pink stall whose sign read: "Arnolf! The Wizard of Candy!" Long ago, the old sign had read: "Arnolf, the Candy Wizard." That was until someone had tried to take a bite out of Arnolf to see if he really was made of candy. In the center of the stall, there stood a large spinning wheel. Huge strands of taffy stretched and squished as they were bent and folded by the motion of the wheel. Stuck upon the taffy, spinning wildly head over heels with the wheel, was a screaming man in an all white uniform.

"Arnolf must have a new apprentice," grinned Torfulson, resuming his journey.

Though Torfulson's stomach encouraged him to tarry and enjoy some treats, his brain refused for he had no leisure time to shop and eat. Farmer Jennix had been quite clear on that.

"Get ya arse straight to the blacksmith," the crotchety farmer had commanded earlier. "Then straight back with my new hinges. We're putting them on yet today. Now shake a leg."

Clang *Clang* *Clang* Rang out the sound of the blacksmith's hammer hitting iron. The sound called out to Torfulson, signaling his quest's destination. Briskly, Torfulson hurried across the street towards the blacksmith's open air shop.

A shallow weather beaten roof provided shade for the shop beneath. An assortment of horseshoes and iron tools hung from the roof's low hanging rafters. Waves of heat rolled off of the immense forge which dominated the shop's center. A burly blacksmith, hammer in hand, stood at the anvil besides the forge, diligently working a piece of metal.

"Can I help you, son?" inquired the blacksmith, looking up from his anvil as Torfulson approached.

Torfulson nodded, "I'm here to pick up some barn hinges for farmer Jennix."

With large metal tongs, the blacksmith lifted a flat piece of metal from the anvil.

"I'm working on them right now. It'll probably be a few more minutes. This dwarven iron has been a royal pain in the butt to work with."

"What makes it dwarven iron?" curiously asked Torfulson. "I mean, what properties does it contain that regular iron doesn't."

"It was sold by a dwarf," blankly replied the blacksmith.

"Ok..." mumbled Torfulson.

The blacksmith hammered the hinge a few more times, then let out an angry curse.

"Oh poofleflaf! This is the worst. I've gotta heat this metal every two seconds it seems. Ughh...."

Angrily, the blacksmith shoved the stubborn metal into the heart of the forge with his tongs.

"Then why do you use dwarven iron?" inquired Torfulson.

"I get it cheap. No one else in town can work it. I can only work it, cause of this."

The blacksmith stepped over toward a massive wooden frame which rested near the forge. The thick timbers of the frame held up a giant bellows made of wood, leather, and shining brass. It was the largest bellows that Torfulson had ever seen. The black smith reached up and grabbed a chain, which was attached to one end of the bellows. As he pulled and slackened the chain, the bellows began to pump. A slight wheeze escaped the bellows into the fiery forge. In a second, the wheeze turned into the mighty roar of forced air. As the air rushed over the forge's coals, they glowed bright red.

"Those bellows are huge," gasped Torfulson.

"Yup," replied the blacksmith, beaming with pride. "They're the largest bellows in the entire kingdom."

"They must blow a lot of air."

"Of course they do, son," smiled the blacksmith. "As my wife says, they're an even bigger windbag than I am!"

"Do you think you could reverse them? Make them suck instead?"

The blacksmith stopped for a moment deep in thought as the bellows roared beside him. Torfulson's question was a problem that he had never thought of before, and he liked solving problems.

"Well..." began the blacksmith. "I don't know why anyone would do that. Sorta defeats the purpose of them and all, but, I guess, if'n you inverted the valve, make the in, the out, you might just reverse the flow and make it suck air."

Torfulson clapped his hands in eager joy. It was the answer that he had wanted to hear.

"Where can I get a set of bellows that big?" excitedly inquired Torfulson. "Would you sell them?"

"Nope, not in a million years," chuckled the blacksmith. "I had them custom made ages ago by a guy way out in West Chester. Set me back almost four thousand gold guilders."

"That's more money than most folks make in a lifetime," dejectedly sighed Torfulson.

"Yup, but it's been worth it. I can usually work twice as fast as I used to with my old bellows. And it's the only way I can work this ding dong dwarven iron. Hinges."

"Hinges on what?" confusedly asked Torfulson.

The blacksmith smiled as he pulled the red hot metal from the forge and placed it upon his anvil. With a few more experienced hits, he finished crafting them into shape. Then he doused the hinge into a nearby bucket of water. A moment later he assembled the hinges, then held them up for Torfulson to see.

"Not too bad, if I do say so myself," crowed the blacksmith. "And they'll last you a lot longer than ones you'd get else where. Now, that'll be two gold."

Torfulson reached into his pocket and absentmindedly pulled out the two gold guilders that farmer Jennix had sent with him. The blacksmith eagerly took the gold, then placed the finished barn door hinges into Torfulson's hands.

"Pleasure doing business," stated the blacksmith before hurrying off to help other customers.

"Mmmhmmm," absentmindedly whispered Torfulson.

His eyes were dead set upon the massive bellows.

CHAPTER 10: BRAINSTORM

Torfulson's brain buzzed excitedly with possibility while the dairy farm's persistent flies buzzed all around him. The hours since he'd returned to work with the new barn hinges seemed to move at a glacial pace, but time, like glaciers, eventually moves. The second his work shift was over, he hastily threw his bag over his shoulder and began to jog towards the King's Highway.

"I hope they're still open," he impatiently whispered to himself.

A passerby would have been forgiven for assuming that the rushing young man was attempting to beat the encroaching storm clouds that were advancing in on the city. Torfulson, though, had taken little notice of the coming tempest. Lost in thought, he sped along the highway, through Oppidium's main gate into the heart of the city. Once more he returned to the market district.

The market square was much emptier than it had been earlier in the day. A number of shop keeps were actively closing down their stalls for the night. On the edge of the market square, there stood an old decrepit store which tilted slightly to the side. A wooden placard hung upon two stout rusty chains above the store's front door. The sign was carved into the shape of a quill pen upon a piece of paper. Painted on the sign in flaking gold paint was the word "Glenda's." A small bell rang, as Torfulson pushed opened the store's front door and entered.

"Welcome to Glenda's stationery store," greeted the friendly shop keep. "You can always find us here, because we don't move."

The shop keep watched Torfulson intently to see if he got her little joke. The joke flew over his head as he flew over to the shelves. A cluster of pencils sat in a glass jar upon the shelf. Torfulson indiscriminately grabbed two at once, then turned towards the shop keep's counter across the store.

"Do you have any paper... uh... like really big paper?"

"Going to write a really big letter?" asked Glenda with sly smile.

"No."

Torfulson's short answer had not meant to be rude. It was the kind of short answer one gives when they are distractedly focused on a singular thing. The shop keep pointed to the far corner of the room. There, in a midsized barrel, lay a handful of four foot tall pieces of paper rolled up like massive scrolls.

"Perfect!" smiled Torfulson as his gaze fell upon the paper.

In a flash, he retrieved one of the massive scrolls then lay it and the pencils upon the shop keep's counter. The distant sounds of rolling thunder grew closer as the shop keep quickly bound the paper and pencils with a piece of string. The sounds of coins clinking in payment upon the counter were followed by the sound of the shop's door bell ringing once more. Torfulson emerged from the shop, purchases in hand, and began to rush home while flashes of distant lightning began to fill the dark sky. He had just set foot into his hovel, when the first drops of rain began to fall.

Eagerly, he placed his purchases upon his weathered table, then looked around for a knife. There, upon his bent fireplace mantle, under a layer of dust, lay the carving knife that he'd had since childhood. Wasting no time, he quickly grabbed the knife, cutting the string which bound his purchases. Next, he unrolled the large piece of paper onto his table. Then, carving knife in hand, he carefully sharpened tips onto both pencils. After which, he sat down on a wobbly stool and proceeded to get to work.

As the hours passed, the storm over the city grew in strength. Sheets of rain poured onto the buildings below. Gangs of homeless children complained about it not being bath time. The streets became shallow rivers coursing throughout the city, and the sewers filled to their brims.

Several sewer alligators even briefly swam out of sewer grates and into the city's streets in search of prey. Most, though, beat a hasty retreat to the safety of the sewers after encountering gangs of violent young children who wanted to use them as bath toys. Even for a vicious Oppidium sewer gator, some things are too much.

Lightning flashed and thunder roared, shaking buildings throughout the city. At 10:04 pm, a bolt of lightning shot down from the heavens, striking Oppidium's massive clock tower. The gnomes, who worked in the clock tower, fled from the building covered in flames. Their screams and burning clothes were quickly drenched as they plunged themselves into the rivers of water that covered the streets. Though the gnomes would all survive, the young gnome Wembly's eyebrows would never grow back.

Though Torfulson's shack shook all around him, he took little notice of it. He was too busy drawing, writing, and planning his new and improved milking contraption. He was so entrenched in his work that he didn't even hear the first knock on his front door, but he certainly did hear the second. The second knock threatened to throw the door off of its very hinges.

It was then that Torfulson came to his senses and looked around the room. He now heard the pouring rain landing on the shack's roof and the earth shaking peals of thunder all around him.

"Who could be coming to visit on such a horrid night?" he wondered aloud.

Not only that, but Torfulson seldom had visitors. He heard a third knock which was even harder than the first two. His front door buckled and shook at the blow.

"Alright! Alright! I'm coming," shouted Torfulson. "Don't break my door down!"

The wobbly stool scrapped across the wood floor as Torfulson stood up and slid it out from under him. Then he grabbed his fireplace poker with one hand and hid it behind himself. It was better to be safe than sorry in Oppidium. Slowly, he walked across the small room to the front door. Cautiously, he gripped the door's handle with his free hand. Nervously, he turned the handle, opening the door just enough to peak out. There he saw a drenched hairy homeless man.

The rain had drenched Menderchuck through and through. It dripped from his overgrown hair. It dripped from his beard. It had been such a long journey to get here; but here he finally stood, outside of a small hovel waiting for her to answer. The door creaked opened a bit, and a young man peered out at him instead. There was an awkward pause as the two men stared at each other. Menderchuck felt a fool. He'd spent months getting here, and he hadn't even planned on what to say.

"I don't have any money," lied Torfulson.

"What?" asked a confused Menderchuck. "I don't need money... well... I mean we all need money... but that's not why I'm here."

Menderchuck had no problem charging a host of enemy archers or stalking a wolf for its pelt, but this was a more troublesome sort of opponent, emotions. He steeled himself.

"Lorelei," Menderchuck almost whispered. "Does she still live here?"

Instantly Torfulson's demeanor changed. He leaned the fireplace poker against the wall and turned towards the drenched man. He studied Menderchuck's face. It seemed a bit familiar, but he was sure that he had never seen it before. His mother had had lot's of male friends who had stayed with them over the years, but this certainly wasn't one of them. Menderchuck shuffled his weight from one side to the other in the awkward silence.

"Lorelei," repeated Menderchuck. "I think she used to live here. Does she still live here?"

"No," coldly replied Torfulson.

As the rain rolled pitilessly down Menderchuck, he sighed deeply. He'd spent months getting here just for her, and she was gone. How was he going to find her in this teeming metropolis? He'd never even seen a city this large before.

"Thanks anyways," dejectedly sighed Menderchuck, before turning away from the door.

"She's dead," replied Torfulson with a heavy tinge of sadness in his voice. "The plague got her a few years back."

Menderchuck stopped in his tracks as a wave of emotion crashed over him. His shoulders slumped in despair. All was lost. He had come too late. After a moment, he heard Torfulson speak behind him.

"If that's all you need, I have work to get back to."

Menderchuck nodded silently, then remembered something. He turned back towards Torfulson, reached into his jerkin, and pulled out an old yellowed letter. The letter, unlike the drenched barbarian, was dry. He pushed the letter into Torfulson's hands.

"Is there any chance you know of a guy named Torfulson?" desperately asked Menderchuck. "The letter shows how his name is spelled, if that helps."

"How does this grubby hobo know my name?" silently thought an alarmed Torfulson, taken a back by the unexpected sound of his own name. "Is this some sort of scam?"

The letter crinkled as Torfulson opened it. There on the parchment, to his surprise, was the writing of his mother Lorelei. He would recognize it anywhere. Especially the silly little hearts she would write over lowercase i's.

Rain continued to pour down on Menderchuck as Torfulson read the letter in the relative dryness of the doorway. As he read, his eyes grew large with surprise. Incredulously, Torfulson looked down at the letter, then up at Menderchuck, then down at the letter, then back up at Menderchuck.

"Noooo, no, this can't be," said Torfulson out loud.

"What?" asked a thoroughly confused Menderchuck.

"You're my... ffff... ff... father?"

A smile crept onto Menderchuck's face.

"Torfulson! I finally found you! Now let me get out of this rain. What do you have to eat?"

Menderchuck pushed past Torfulson and entered the shack. Torfulson stood slack jawed by the door, letter in hand, staring at the hairy homeless hobo who had just entered his hovel.

CHAPTER 11: YOU'RE MY DAD?

Menderchuck left a trail of water on the floor behind him as he beelined across the room towards the pantry cabinet. Once there, he unceremoniously dropped his sword and war bow to the ground and then threw open the cabinet's doors.

Torfulson hadn't said a single word since Menderchuck had entered the room. Instead he read the old letter, over and over. It was definitely written by his mother.

"My beloved Menderchuck," the letter began. "You are my heart. I write you with the greatest of news, for I have given birth to our son. He is strong and healthy. He has your nose, and the twinkle in your eyes. I have named him Torfulson. Not a day goes by that I do not yearn to have you beside me once again. Though he does not know you yet, I know that our son misses you too. I wish you would leave the clan to Oleg, and come join us here. I now have my own home in the city of Oppidium. It is large and majestic with ample room for us, and many more children."

Torfulson looked skeptically around his decrepit lifelong home. His mother had been a bit liberal in her description of the hovel. He was still too naive to realize that the truth often dies a thousand deaths in a romantic relationship.

The letter continued with heartfelt confessions of love and ended with directions on how to find their home. Torfulson looked up from the letter to the dripping wet Menderchuck, who sat upon the floor in a puddle of water. Menderchuck had an apple in one hand, a loaf of bread in the other, and a combination of both crammed into his busily chewing mouth.

"Merrmpphh," bits of food flew out of Menderchuck's mouth as he tried to talk and eat at the same time.

"What?" asked a confused Torfulson.

Menderchuck swallowed down a mouthful of food, then hacked loudly and grossly as he cleared his throat.

"So, you're my son. Yeah, I can see the resemblance. You look just like me," declared Menderchuck before greedily biting into another mouthful of bread.

Torfulson furrowed his brow slightly in offense. He didn't see the likeness at all. He was slightly tall, while his father was slightly small. He was well groomed and shaved, while his father's hair and beard looked as wild as a thicket. He was skinny and lean, while his father was muscular.

"This... this is a bit much to all take in," stuttered Torfulson. "Where.. Where have you been all my life?"

"Been busy," came Menderchuck's muffled reply while he loudly chewed his food.

"Busy?!" erupted Torfulson, unable to contain

himself.

"Yup," nodded Menderchuck, taking a big bite out of the apple in his hand.

A childhood's worth of pain flashed through Torfulson's eyes in a second. He had grown up fatherless. A point that the taunts and jests of the neighborhood children had often reminded him of.

Though his mother had done everything in her power to provide them with food, shelter, love and support, their life had been a hard one. For years, a young Torfulson had dreamed of meeting his real father whom he knew nothing about.

At times, young Torfulson had dreamed of his father charging in upon a mighty stallion in shiny armor. A heroic knight returned from war. Then his knight father would whisk his mother and him away to a fancy manor house. A mansion of plenty, where stomachs were always full and the cold of winter was kept at bay.

At other times, he dreamed that his father was a mighty pirate captain returned from the sea with chests of gold. Together they would sail the seas in search of high adventure.

And at other times, he had imagined his father to be a mighty wizard who would throw fireballs at those who had mercilessly bullied him in school. This had been a particularly recurrent daydream on tedious school days.

His boyhood dreams had all shared one thing in common. In all of them, his father was tall, strong, majestic and would save him and his mother from a life of poverty. In none of his dreams was his father an indifferent, shortish, dirty, soggy, hairy, homeless man with the table manners of a boar. Yet there he was. Squat on his very floor in his tiny hovel.

"So," asked Menderchuck. "Whadda ya do to earn all this bread? You a thief?"

"No."

"A highway man?"

"No, isn't that the same thing?" asked a perplexed Torfulson.

"You a pirate?"

"No," replied a flustered Torfulson, wondering why his newfound father would assume that he stole things. "If you must know, I'm a milkmaid."

Menderchuck burst into an uproarious laughter which bounced off of the small room's walls competing with the rolling thunder which roared outdoors, but then he suddenly went silent.

"Acckk... Accck...." futilely gasped Menderchuck, grasping at his own throat.

Menderchuck's eyes began to bulge and his face began to turn a shade of purple.

"Stop choking!" blurted out Torfulson, watching

in horror as his father's eyes began to roll back into his head.

Wasting no time, Torfulson sprung into action, darting across the small room. In his haste, he tripped upon his wobbly stool, flying forward. In vain, his arms flailed about trying to regain his balance, but it was too late. He plummeted head first into Menderchuck's gut. The force of Torfulson's face colliding with Menderchuck's stomach caused Menderchuck to lurch forwards. Menderchuck's mouth flew open as a soggy wad of bread shot out of it, landing with a squishy thud only a foot away.

"HHhhhh... Hhhhh..." gasped Menderchuck in relief, filling his lungs with long deep breaths.

With watery eyes, Menderchuck looked over at Torfulson, who now lay on the ground beside him nursing a bruised nose.

"Thanks Torf," gratefully wheezed Menderchuck between labored breathes.

After a moment, Menderchuck looked at the soggy wad of bread which lay on the floor beside him.

"You know," began Menderchuck. "Thousands of warriors have tried to kill me over the years, but only that wad of bread has ever come close to doing it."

"Really?"

"Yup."

Then Menderchuck shrugged his shoulders, picked up the wad of bread, put it back into his mouth, and began chewing it again.

"So Torf, where do I sleep?"

"But I have a million questions for you," protested Torfulson.

Menderchuck nodded, "And you deserve answers, but my road has been very long, and I am very weary. Let me rest now, and tomorrow I will answer any question you have."

CHAPTER 12:
MENDERCHUCK'S DREAM

Menderchuck slept fitfully that night, drifting in and out of a familiar dream. It was the same nightmare that he'd had almost every night since the battle. He stood upon the plains of Rannsaka once again while the night wind blew through his hair.

He looked to the west and was overcome with joy. There, only about twenty yards away, stood his clan. He smiled as he saw his grandmother, his brother, and even his mother. The clan, his family, saw him and smiled back.

"Mother! Mert! Wait for me!" eagerly cried out Menderchuck as began to run towards a joyful reunion with his clan.

But no matter how hard Menderchuck ran, the clan never came any closer. He ran as hard as he could, until his sides hurt, yet the happy clan Chuck was always twenty yards away. And then Menderchuck saw him.

"No...." despondently gasped Menderchuck.

In the distance, even further to the west, was the unmistakable image of Duke Belloch. Clan Chuck stood obliviously between the Duke and Menderchuck. Menderchuck's heart sunk, knowing what would happen next for he'd had this nightmare many times before.

Menderchuck opened his mouth to scream, to

warn the clan of the Duke's impending danger, but no words would escape his mouth. The black night sky turned blood red as Duke Belloch pounced upon the unsuspecting clan. Menderchuck watched in helpless horror as the Duke first butchered the clan's men, then the women, and finally the helpless children.

The Duke's armor ran red with the blood of the innocent, and his eyes glowed a hellish red. Threateningly, he turned towards Menderchuck and opened his mouth, revealing row after row of sharp pointed teeth. Then the Duke spoke.

"Hey, Menderchuck. I gotta go to work."

Menderchuck was confused. The Duke had never said that before in the dream.

"Menderchuck," repeated Torfulson, shaking Menderchuck awake.

Menderchuck rubbed his eyes, then opened them, "What?"

Torfulson threw his work bag over his shoulder. Earlier, he had hidden his life savings inside of it. It wasn't that he didn't trust the father that he'd just met the night before. It was just... yeah, he didn't trust him yet.

"I gotta go to work," repeated Torfulson. "There's still some food in the pantry, if you're hungry. Well, unless you ate it all last night. When I get back tonight, I'll take you to the best restaurant in town, and then you can answer my questions. Don't leave me, errr, here, until then.

Deal?"

Menderchuck nodded in the way one does when they've just woken up and are still a bit confused.

"Oh, and you might want to take a bath before we go," suggested Torfulson as he stepped out the door and headed off to work.

CHAPTER 13: THE DUKE

As dawn broke over the teeming metropolis of Oppidium, it had already been light for several hours in the far off rustic village of Novsh. Novsh stood far far away from Oppidium, across hill and dale, deep in the flat wide plains of the Steppes of Rannsaka.

Stood isn't the correct word though. The small village of Novsh leaned. The village's crude sod huts leaned lazily to the side, as though standing was too much effort. Wood, you see, was a rare commodity in this part of the Steppes; and thus most of the village's buildings were made of sod. The village's few wood constructs consisted of a handful of drab market stalls that filled its pitiful market square.

On this particular day, a few of the gaunt and dirty villagers of Novsh were busy perusing the sparse market stalls for deals. A bald man looked down at a clump of hair which rested upon a counter in a market stall.

"Used hair, one copper?!" cried out the bald man in an offended tone. "Who would ever pay so much?! That's highway robbery."

The merchant just looked at the bald man and smiled. He'd dealt with enough customers in the past to know that despite his complaints, the bald man would be buying this clump of used hair.

"It looks like dirty cat fur!" complained the bald man.

It was true. It had taken the merchant quite some time to trap the cat, and it had been absolutely filthy. It had taken him even longer to shave the cat, and his wife had derided him for it.

"You fool, it's a waste of time shaving a dirty cat."

"Is that why you don't shave your mustache?" the merchant had asked her in flippant response.

Needless to say, an argument ensued. By the time it was over, the merchant had been banished to the couch for the night which gave him plenty of time and space to finish shaving the cat.

"No one would ever pay that much!" cried out the bald man again as he pulled a copper out of his pocket and placed it upon the merchant's counter.

Then the bald man picked up the clump of dirty cat fur and hurriedly walked away. He hastily ducked down an alleyway and placed the dirty cat fur upon his head. For a moment, he fiddled with it until it felt right. Then he proudly strutted back into the market square with a clump of dirty cat fur upon his head.

"Who does he think he's fooling?" sighed the Duke, shaking his head and watching on from a short distance away.

Duke Belloch stood alone in the center of the market square. He also stood out like a sore thumb. Unlike the gaunt and dirty villagers, he was well fed and clean. His hair was trimmed, and his face was shaved clean. His tunic was a strong royal blue, and he wore a long golden hilted sword upon his leather belt which was fastened by a shining brass buckle. In one hand, he held some sort of fried meat on a stick.

"Ugggh," grunted the Duke, studying the questionable meat and gently poking at it with his free hand. "What kind of meat is this even? Rat? Ewww, I'm not risking it."

Disgusted, Duke Belloch released the meat stick from his hand. As it landed upon the ground with a small squishy thud, the Duke gazed at the square around him. The truth is that he had only bought the fried meat to try and make some headway with the ignorant locals, but it wasn't working. The locals kept their distance, staring at him.

"Ughhhh," sighed Duke Belloch. "This isn't how it was supposed to go."

His official title was Duke Belloch of Rivolli. He ruled a prosperous duchy on the far edge of the kingdom, near the western edges of the Steppes of Rannsaka. The Steppes, though, knew no king. They were wild untamed lands inhabited by independent towns that were separated by miles of plains.

Over the centuries, many foolish kings had tried to invade the Steppes. Each seeing the independent towns as easy pickings, but none of the invaders had ever planned for the horse clans.

The horse clans were both the bane and the boon

of the Steppes. Ruthless nomadic raiders known across the plains for their skills at riding and at archery. The various clans troubled the towns with their frequent raids, but, by the same measure, they protected the towns' independence by destroying any invading armies.

The armies of the west were just not built to combat the speed, accuracy, and range of the clans' deadly horse archers. And in the clans, everyone was a horse archer. The clans had one fatal weakness though, they were divided.

Like the failed kings of old, Duke Belloch was ambitious and wished to conquer the Steppes for himself. Unlike the kings of old, Duke Belloch had studied history.

"The key," he had reasoned. "Is to exploit their weakness, their division. I don't need a massive army that outnumbers all the clans. I just need enough men to out number each clan individually, and fight them one by one."

He had planned it all out. Unlike kings past, he wouldn't foolishly chase the horse clans, allowing them to use their advantages in speed. Instead, through guile and subterfuge, he would trick the clans into coming to him one at a time. Though the battles would be on the Steppes, Duke Belloch would chose where he met each and every clan.

And once he had destroyed the horse clans that had raided and plagued the independent towns of the Steppes, then those grateful towns would welcome him as their new savior, protector, and liege lord.

"All hail king me," the Duke had often whispered in prophetic fantasy.

Sure, he reasoned, there would most likely be a small number of ungrateful peasants who would resist and need some convincing. Perhaps they would have to be introduced to the "red hot poker of reason" or the "rusty metal spikes of compliance," but little did that trouble Duke Belloch, who was well versed in their use. And in the end, all of the independent towns would bend the knee and fall under his rule. He would bring peace, prosperity, safety, infrastructure, and sanitation to the unwashed masses of the Steppes. And in return, they would willingly serve his every wish.

Step 1 had worked flawlessly. The Duke had done the nigh impossible. He had killed or conquered all of the horse clans, but Step 2 was turning out to be much more difficult than he had originally anticipated. The peasant towns were turning out to be surprisingly stubborn. No one had welcomed him gratefully as a savior, a protector, or a liege lord. One by one, he had been forced to conquer each independent town as he had the horse clans. Admittedly, it was much easier to kill unwashed peasants, but that was not the point.

"Hmmph, I deserve some gratitude," pouted the Duke, glaring disdainfully at the village around him.

Yes, he had conquered the towns. Yes, tax

revenue was up. Unwilling up, but up none the less.

"Ungrateful moronic peasants," grumbled Duke Belloch. "They do everything they can to avoid paying taxes, taxes that are for their own good. I bring them the gift of civilization, and they'd rather sit in their own filth like animals."

In Bixby, he had used their tax money to build a great fountain so that all could have fresh water. The fools had just used it as a giant toilet instead, befouling it beyond repair.

In Arphander, he had used their tax money to build a great cobblestone road that no one used. The peasants purposely avoided it, using the old worn dirt roads that they had always used.

In the town of Grand River, he had built a large school to educate the children of the territory, but it sat vacant. Parents refused to let their children go to the school for fear that they'd become indoctrinated in an evil dark government plot involving rye bread.

"Damns fools, I don't even like rye bread!" angrily thought the Duke. "I just want to teach your inbred children to read, to write, to stop marrying their relatives, and to honor the divine right of kings! These are normal things that any civilized society does!"

In the village of Hestings, the Duke had tried to consolidate all of the farmland into one giant farmstead. It, he reasoned, would be much more efficient to have all the farmers working together on a single farm. That way farm equipment could be easily shared amongst a greater number of workers. Not to mention that it would make it easier to implement things like crop rotation and diversity. He had expected that there would be resistance from the bigger farms in the area, but what he hadn't expected was the resistance from the small farms.

"AggghhhH!!!!!" grunted the frustrated Duke.

Dozens of times, to no avail, he had tried to explain to the small farms that by working a giant communal farm their increased combined harvest would more than make up for their personal loss in farmland. He pleaded with their ignorant faces, lecturing them on the potentials of shoring up the whole town against future famines. In fact, the more he tried to convince the farmers that a giant farm was good for the community, the more they doubted him.

Instead he got insolent questions from the peasant farmers like: "What do you get out of this?" "Gimme my land back!" "Were you poopin' in my fields last night?"

Actually he had been, but that was an unrelated problem due to some bad soup that he'd had the night before. It wasn't personal, but the farmer wouldn't believe him. In the end, Duke Belloch had forced the farms to consolidate at sword point. And the minute he had left the village of Hestings, the farmers abandoned the giant farm and returned to their own ways on their own plots of land.

"You going to eat that?"

The unexpected voice of the bald man with the dirty cat hair upon his head distracted the Duke from his thoughts. The bald man stood beside the Duke, pointing down at the fried meat on a stick that lay in the dirt below.

"By all means, help yourself," replied the Duke with a dismissive wave of his hand.

Hungrily, the bald man reached down to grab the fried treat. As he did, the dirty cat hair upon his head began to slide. Reflexively, he slammed a hand down on the top of his head to hold the hair in place. He paused for a brief moment to look around and make sure that no one had noticed.

"Windy day, don't want it messing up my hair," explained the crouched bald man in a transparent   lie.

"Yes, I have the same problem," sarcastically replied the Duke.

With his free hand, the bald man grabbed the meat on a stick and then stood upright. Dirt stuck fast to the sides of the fried food.

"Thanks mister," smiled the bald man before taking a big bite of the dirty meat. "Mmmm, gritty, just the way momma used to make it."

The Duke winced as he watched the bald man wander off eating the dirt covered meat.

"I can't spend all summer in this hick town," sighed the frustrated Duke, talking to himself. "I've dozen of towns to reform and a capital to build. Where's my horse at? Hopefully these morons haven't tried to eat it."

And with that, Duke Belloch turned his back on Novsh and set his sights on the next part of his plan.

CHAPTER 14: THE BATH

"A bath?!" defiantly thought Menderchuck. "Why I just took a bath in the river Golyn a month ago... or was it two... when was it?..."

Earlier in the day as he'd left for work, Torfulson had encouraged his father to take a bath. Now, many hours later, Menderchuck reluctantly lowered his nose towards his own armpit, nostrils flaring as he took a big whiff.

"Whoaaaaa," swooned Menderchuck. "I guess I am a bit ripe."

In short order the barbarian turned the small shack upside down in vain, searching for a bathtub. The most that he found was an old wooden bucket and a sponge.

"Pshhh," scoffed Menderchuck. "That will never hold a man of my girth. I need something bigger."

And so the search for an acceptable bathing receptacle expanded beyond the crowded confines of Torfulson's shack.

On the Steppes of Rannsaka, the horse clans bathed in the Steppes' wild rivers and ponds. Thus Menderchuck began to scout throughout the Oppidium slums for a small pond or river in which to bathe. Unfortunately for him, there were none to be found. In the immediate vicinity, the only body of water, in which he could fit his body, was the horse trough which sat across the street from Torfulson's home.

"It'll do," declared Menderchuck, publicly disrobing and tossing his soiled leather jerkin upon the shack's front stairs.

Boldly, Menderchuck the nude strolled across the muddy street, stopping for a moment beside the trough to look down at its murky waters. Bits of debris floated upon its surface. It seemed unlikely that the water was changed often, but this didn't stop Menderchuck in the least.

"Feel the wrath of my bath!" exclaimed Menderchuck aloud as he enthusiastically leapt into the horse trough with a mighty splash.

With a smile, Menderchuck leaned back, relaxing in the horse water and waving cordially at passersby while he publicly bathed. Disgusted neighbors hurried past, shielding their eyes from the offensive view. Well, most did. Admittedly, a few passersby snuck in curious sidelong glances at the strange foreigner who was bathing in the neighborhood horse trough.

It was hard to say who got the worse end of the bath, Menderchuck or the horse water. As Menderchuck climbed out of the trough, he left a thin layer of grease upon the water. Later in the evening, more than one member of the neighborhood would be confused when they led their horse to the trough for a drink and it refused. Thus reinforcing the old Oppidium axiom, "You can lead a horse to water, but you can't make it drink filthy human tainted water."

Soon, a naked and wet Menderchuck stood alone inside of Torfulson's small decrepit shack. His drenched wild long hair and frizzled beard clung to his head while water dripped off of his body and onto the shack's rough floor.

"Towel?" grunted Menderchuck.

For a moment, the barbarian made a lazy cursory examination of the room, then he gave up and headed into the shack's tiny bed room. Roughly, Menderchuck tore the blankets off of Torfulson's modest bed, wrapping them around his body and drying himself with them. Then he unceremoniously dropped the damp blankets upon the floor and dressed himself once again in his soiled leather jerkin. And not a moment too soon.

"I'm home!" echoed out Torfulson's voice from the shack's main room.

Menderchuck stepped from the bedroom into the main room to see his son.

"Excellent! You bathed!" exclaimed Torfulson upon seeing Menderchuck's still wet hair.

Privately, Torfulson's nose was surprised to notice that Menderchuck still smelled very much like horse.

"You can't wear that, though," groaned Torfulson, pointing at Menderchuck's soiled jerkin.

"Why not?" protested Menderchuck. "It's good

and strong."

"That maybe," replied Torfulson. "But where I'm taking you, there's a dress code."

"I'm not going to wear a dress! I'm not a girl!"

Torfulson shook his head and sped by Menderchuck, disappearing into the small bedroom for a moment. When Torfulson returned, he held a pair of wool clothes in his hands that were identical to the ones that he currently wore.

"Ummm," sputtered Torfulson. "Do you know why my blankets are on the floor... and are wet?"

"You probably peed the bed last night," dryly replied Menderchuck.

"I did not!" fumed Torfulson, before regaining his composure. "Well, anyway, try these on."

Skeptically, Menderchuck took the clothes and disappeared into the bedroom. A few moments later found Menderchuck a changed man, literally. Menderchuck wore the slightly baggy clothes upon his body and a disappointed look upon his face. Upon his back he wore his mighty war bow, and upon his belt he wore his legendary sword Arbjak and his white bone handle knife.

"You look great! Love the style!" encouraged Torfulson, who wasn't the least bit unbiased as he was really complimenting his own clothing.

Menderchuck looked down doubtfully at the

clothes, feeling like a little brother who was wearing his big brother's hand me downs.

"And," continued Torfulson a bit more reluctantly. "You'll have to leave the weapons behind."

"What?" incredulously replied Menderchuck. "What if we are assaulted by brigands, or war parties?"

"We're in the city, we'll be fine. And, more importantly, they don't allow weapons where we're going."

Warily, Menderchuck pulled the war bow off of his back and set it against the wall. Then he removed his white bone handle knife and placed it upon the room's small table. But when he went to remove his sword he faltered.

"Even Arbjak?" timidly asked Menderchuck.

"What's an Arbjak?"

"Behold the blade of legend!" shouted Menderchuck, pulling the blade from its scabbard and holding it high.

Unfortunately for all involved, the ceiling of the small shack was low. The tip of the blade stuck hard and fast into the wood ceiling above with an audible "thunk."

"Ohhh, ummm, uhhhh, sorry bout the ceiling," sheepishly apologized Menderchuck, trying in vain to free the blade .

Menderchuck released the sword's handle, yet it stubbornly hung from the ceiling.

"It's ok..." sighed Torfulson, looking up at the sword.

"Fear not!" boldly declared Menderchuck. "I shall free the blade of legend!"

Menderchuck's hands darted up, grasping Arbjak's handle once more. The muscles on his arms and the veins on his face began to bulge in struggle. Middle aged man groans escaped Menderchuck's lips while he wrestled with the sword. Yet the saber's tip remained steadfastly embedded in the ceiling above.

"Get free, you ding dong donkey poo!" exclaimed Menderchuck, wildly flailing and lurching about.

The more he flailed, the more his long wet hair flew around his head spraying water throughout the room.

"Stop! It's ok! Don't worry about the sword," commanded Torfulson, attempting to shield himself from the hair water that rained around him. "We can take care of the sword when we get back! I think first though, we need to get you to a barber, and then we'll go eat."

Menderchuck's mood improved at the very mention of eating. Instantly, he released the hilt of the blade named Arbjak. Then, with smiles on both men's faces, they walked out of the front door in search of a barber. As the shack's door slammed shut behind them, the blade Arbjak fell from the ceiling and clattered to the floor below.

CHAPTER 15: THE BARBER

Like a younger brother following his older brother through busy hallways on his first day of school, Menderchuck stuck close to Torfulson, following him as he hurriedly pushed his way through the bustling crowds on the King's Highway. With curious eyes, Menderchuck gawked at the mass of traveling peasants, some on foot and some in carts, that filled the busy thoroughfare around them.

"Wow," rubely remarked Menderchuck. "Look at all the dumb clothing styles they wear, and those carts, and those saddles! It's so foreign... and stupid."

"Actually you're the foreigner," brusquely replied Torfulson, stopping short. "We're here."

Torfulson came to a abrupt stop outside of a shop. A large wood sign swung slowly in the wind above the shop's front door. Upon the sign were a moderately competent painted image of a razor blade and the word "Barber" in faded purple letters. Menderchuck, though, took little notice of the sign above for his eyes were apprehensively transfixed upon the large white pole that was draped with bloody towels which stood beside the shop's front door.

Without so much as a word, Torfulson pushed open the shop door and entered. As he did, the door hit a small bell causing it to ring slightly. Menderchuck followed close behind. There he beheld a sight that was even more foreign to him.

In the middle of the shop, there stood two metal chairs that rested upon swivels which could be turned in any direction. An elderly woman currently sat in one of the chairs while the other sat empty. Next to the woman, there stood a slightly balding middle aged man. He wore a friendly smile upon his face and a white overcoat, that was stained with many a blood red spot, upon his body.

"Torfulson!" exclaimed the balding man in friendly greeting. "How good it is to see you. Give me a minute to finish up here, and then I'll be right with you."

Torfulson smiled, nodded, and then took a seat in one of the many chairs that ran in a line along the room's east wall. Absentmindedly, he picked up a small picture book from a pile of books that rested upon a tiny nearby table.

"Oh that's last month's issue," commented the balding barber. "You should really check out this month's issue of 'Goblin Illustrated.' It's on the side of the pile. It's got an interview with Koblar the goblin king, quite fascinating. They don't eat near as many people as you'd think."

"Thanks," responded Torfulson as he began to fish around in the pile of books for the issue of 'Goblin Illustrated.'

Sheepishly, Menderchuck took a seat beside Torfulson, looking around the room in a mixture of wonder and worry.

The shop's far wall, behind the metal chairs, was

a wide giant mirror above a waist high shelf. Upon the shelf, there rested odd creepy jars of large size. Jars of green liquid lay next to jars of red which lay next to jars of purple. Strange metal devices lay in some of the jars. In others; legless, eyeless, armless creatures of small size wriggled about.

The balding man in the white coat strolled over to one such jar and opened it. Then he picked up a pair of rusty metal tongs from the shelf and plunged them into the jar. For a moment he struggled with one of the many creatures which inhabited the jar. Then, victoriously, he pulled the tongs from the jar. Clasped firmly in the tongs' grip, the captured creature wriggled and squirmed.

"Excellent," confidently declared the barber. "This one looks very hungry."

Then the barber scurried over to the elderly lady who lay reclined in one of the two metal chairs. Thin and pale, the woman looked as though most of the color had drained from her body.

"It's a good thing you got here when you did, Mrs. Henderson," consoled the barber in his most reassuring voice. "Forgive me for saying this, but you look like death warmed over. I fear we're going to need to double your blood letting sessions."

Menderchuck grimaced with revulsion, watching the barber place the long slimy black leech upon the old woman with his rusty tongs. Then the barber carefully placed the tongs back upon the shelf, walked over to a wash basin, and washed his hands, drying them upon a blood stained towel.

"Sorry about that, Torfulson," explained the barber in a hushed tone as he approached the waiting men. "Mrs. Henderson's health just hasn't been good since her husband Bert passed away last year. She just needs another decent blood letting. Soooo, what can I do for you and your friend?"

"This is my... my.... Menderchuck," stumbled Torfulson, gesturing towards Menderchuck.

"Father, I'm his father," finished Menderchuck.

"Yeah..." awkwardly agreed Torfulson. "He needs a haircut and a shave."

"Nice to meet you Menderchuck," beamed the barber, placing a friendly hand upon Menderchuck's shoulder. "Right this...."

"Bert, is that you?!" shouted out the old woman at no one in particular.

"I haven't seen you in years," loudly continued the old woman. "Not since you died in that house fire. I certainly didn't expect to see you here today."

"Right this way..." the barber tried to say to Menderchuck again, but his words were interrupted by the old lady once again.

"No, I haven't put on weight, Bert!" exclaimed

the old woman. "How rude of you! And no, my harlot of a sister never liked you."

"Just a moment please," declared the barber, politely excusing himself.

The barber walked over to the mirrored wall and picked up a small rag off of the waist high shelf. He then opened a jar of green liquid and gingerly placed the rag into the liquid. Once the rag was good and drenched, the barber retrieved it and walked over to the metal chair which held the old lady.

"I don't care what you think, Bert," deliriously continued the old woman. "I still say my nephews look a bit like poodles..."

The woman's words trailed off as the barber clasped the damp rag upon her face. The old woman struggled violently for a moment against the barber's firm grasp, but then went limp. The barber smiled, clapped his hands eagerly, and turned back towards Menderchuck.

"Excellent, she's going to have a nice long rest while we get to work."

The barber gestured to the open metal chair in the middle of the room.

"Come take a seat Mr. Menderchuck. We'll get you your shave and a haircut, but could I also interest you in a good blood letting?"

With terrified eyes, Menderchuck looked towards Torfulson, who was also gesturing

Menderchuck towards the metal chair. Thus Menderchuck the Terrible, the once great bold warlord of the Steppes of Rannsaka, timidly walked towards the metal chair. He paused for a reluctant moment beside the chair before relenting and sitting upon it. Jollily, the barber picked up a small thick blanket and placed it upon Menderchuck's torso.

"So about that blood letting?" inquired the barber again.

"Nah, I'm good," squeaked Menderchuck's voice.

"Just hear me out, then you can say no if you want to," continued the barber trying to upsell the barbarian. "Blood letting is the pinnacle of modern science. Nine out of ten barbers agree."

"That's convenient," whispered Menderchuck under his breath, but the barber took no notice.

"Blood letting can cure all manner of discomforts," continued the barber's sales pitch. "Do you suffer from incontinence, muscle aches, head aches, upset stomach, evil spirits, low self esteem, high self esteem, rabies, extreme flatulence, impaired libido, or excessive libido? A good blood letting can cure all of these, and much more."

The barber paused after his spiel, eagerly awaiting Menderchuck's response.

"Nah... I'm good."

"Very well," smiled the barber. "A shave and a hair cut it is. Good to see you already washed your hair."

And with that, the barber walked again over to the mirrored wall. Only this time, he pulled a pair of scissors out of a jar of orange liquid. Then he returned to Menderchuck and began to cut his long wet hair.

Torfulson, who sat across the room reading 'Goblin Illustrated,' never even heard the snip, snip, snip of the scissors. He was much too engrossed in reading: "the ten best things a goblin likes to eat." The barber had been right. To Torfulson's surprise, people were not number one on the list. After a bit though, his reading was rudely interrupted.

"Torfulson... Torfulson, a little help," frantically pleaded the barber.

Torfulson looked up and was shocked to see his father firmly gripping the scared barber. Menderchuck's left hand was wrapped around the barber's neck while his right hand tightly clenched the barber's right wrist which held a long straight edge razor blade.

"It's ok Menderchuck," reassured Torfulson. "He's not an assassin. He's not going to kill you."

Menderchuck loosened his grip on the barber.

"He's just going to shave your beard off," explained Torfulson.

The barber winced as Menderchuck's grasp tightened.

"No," firmly declared Menderchuck.

"Come on," pleaded Torfulson. "Clean shaven, it's the style. And where we're going you need to be decent."

"But then I'd look like you."

Torfulson's brow furrowed slightly, "Is there something wrong with that?"

"Yeah," replied Menderchuck. "I don't want to look like a girl."

Torfulson let out an exasperated sigh, "Fine." Then he turned towards the barber, "Could you just trim his beard instead? Even if it's going to look stupid."

The barber nodded rapidly. Menderchuck, having seen that his beard would be protected in at least some form, released the barber, who then set to work trimming it with his scissors. After a few minutes time, the barber's work was done.

"Excellent, excellent," beamed the barber, looking upon Menderchuck's now well groomed face and head.

Then he turned the metal chair so that it faced the mirror wall.

"Welllll?" asked the barber. "What do you think?"

Menderchuck's body language slumped as he viewed himself in the mirror, "I look like a dork. I want to raid myself now..."

"Nonsense," cheerily remarked Torfulson, walking up to the two men. "Other than the beard you look great. And even the beard looks so much better trimmed."

Then the barber walked over to one of the many jars that sat upon his waist high shelf. This one was full of hard peppermint candies. He took one out and handed it to Menderchuck.

"For being such a good sitter," smiled the barber. "Now that'll be two copper for the shave and a hair cut."

Menderchuck greedily shoved the candy into his mouth and began to suck on it.

"Mmmmm, I donff hafff any munnny," mumbled the barbarian.

Confused, the barber looked over to Torfulson. Torfulson rolled his eyes and proceeded to take two copper coins from his pocket, placing them in the barber's outstretched hand. And with that, the three men exchanged goodbyes. The barber waved a friendly farewell as the door closed behind the two men.

"Nice kid, odd father," uttered the barber to himself. "So, Mrs. Henderson, how are you..."

As the barber turned toward the old lay who limply lay in the metal chair, he abruptly stopped in mid-sentence. There he beheld the slimy black leech that he had laid upon her earlier. It still fed from the old lady's arm, but had now grown to over ten times its original size.

"Oh dear, oh dear!" lamented the barber in a hurried rush. "Let's get that off of you."

CHAPTER 16: THE RESTAURANT

Torfulson and Menderchuck stood awkwardly in the waiting room of the restaurant Immundus while the sounds of tinking silverware, moderate conversation, and the smells of baked food wafted in from the nearby dining room. Instinctively, Menderchuck's left hand moved to his waist in an attempt to rest upon his sword's pommel. His hand found no purchase though, instead whiffing clumsily by his side.

"You should have let me bring Arbjak," sulked Menderchuck, missing his trusty blade.

Menderchuck shuffled his feet like a bored child and began to look around the waiting room. The waiting room's walls were covered with a gaudy red and gold wallpaper. Several mostly clean leather couches sat unused along one of the waiting room's walls. Menderchuck's eyes drifted down to the thick royal violet carpeting which surrounded his feet. It, like the rest of the building, seemed a bit past its prime.

"I've seen outhouses with nicer carpeting," mumbled Menderchuck.

"What? You don't like this place?" asked Torfulson with a hurt look in his eye. "When I was young, Mom used to bring me here on my birthdays... when we could afford it. I wanted to be able to share that with you."

"I love this place, it's great," lied Menderchuck suddenly aware of his accidental offense. "I just...

uh... so Lorelei took you here?"

"Yes."

"Well I can see why," the words stumbled out of Menderchuck's mouth like a drunk leaving a bar. "She always had great taste... except in carpeting. I'm glad to be here."

A moderately attractive waitress entered the waiting room and beckoned to the two men.

"Please follow me, sirs."

"Oh thank the gods," sighed Menderchuck aloud.

"What, sir?" asked the woman.

"I love this place!" shouted out Menderchuck as he entered the dining room, turning quite a few heads to Torfulson's embarrassment.

Obediently, Menderchuck and Torfulson followed the waitress into the heart of the busy dining room, passing tables full of hungry eaters.

"This is your table, gentlemen," explained the waitress, gesturing to a small table beside them.

"Thank you," shyly responded Torfulson, pulling a chair out from under the table and taking a seat.

"Look out food, here I come! In my belly and out my bum," loudly declared Menderchuck while he roughly pulled his chair out from under the table.

Menderchuck's chair flew backward, accidentally hitting the back of the chair of a nearby corpulent man. Unfortunately for the corpulent man, he was holding a bowl of steaming hot soup in his hands that he was blowing on to cool. As the two chairs collided, the corpulent man was rudely pushed forward, causing the bowl of hot soup to slip from his hands.

"WaoooOOWWWW!" painfully yelled out the corpulent man as the steaming hot soup poured into his lap.

Menderchuck looked back at the corpulent man, and then gave him a friendly slap on the back.

"You gotta be careful there, bud," sympathized Menderchuck. "That soup looks hot."

With fury in his eyes, the corpulent man looked up to give Menderchuck a dirty look, but by then it was too late. Menderchuck had already plopped down in his own chair at his own table with his back to the corpulent man.

"We'll take two thick crust meat pies, with heavy sides of mashed potatoes and gravy, please," bashfully requested Torfulson.

The waitress nodded, then walked away. As soon as she was out of ear shot, Torfulson excitedly pointed to the cloth upon their table.

"Check it out! They have real cloth table... uh clothes. And look at the silver ware."

Torfulson picked up a fork and held it up for Menderchuck to see.

"Ummm.... it's clean?" guessed Menderchuck taking a stab in the dark at what Torfulson was alluding too.

"Exactly! And so are the cups! This place is the best, and just wait til you've tried the food."

While Torfulson joyfully beheld the restaurant ambiance around him, Menderchuck scanned the room, feeling a heavy fall from grace. Wealthy merchant men, wearing fine waist coats and gilded tights, clinked the golden rings upon their fingers while they greedily ate their steaks. Exquisite women, wearing fine lace dresses and sparkling jewel encrusted necklaces, gossiped about the newest scandals between bites of food.

A year ago, Menderchuck would have been raiding a place such as this on the plains far away. The rich and fat would have been turning their valuables over to him. But now he had been brought low, just another customer buying a meal.

"Questions," lightly coughed Torfulson, disturbing the table's silence.

"Yes, yes," smiled Menderchuck. "I promised answers to all your questions, or at least those I can answer. Fire away."

"What is your occupation?"

Blankly, Menderchuck stared back at Torfulson.

"Ummm... what do you do for a living?" tried Torfulson, rephrasing the question.

"I was the chief of clan Chuck. The greatest of the horse raider clans of the Steppes of Rannsaka."

"You're a barbarian?!" excitedly gasped Torfulson.

"That's not the word we would use for it, but yes."

The two men's nascent conversation was cut short as the waitress returned with two plates. Each plate held a steaming hot golden crusted meat pie and a massive pile of creamy mashed potatoes that were drenched in a river of gravy. Carefully, she placed a plate in front of each man, then filled their cups with a bottle of the house wine.

"I hope you enjoy your food," she kindly declared before walking away.

Torfulson's enamored eyes followed her as she left the table. This did not escape Menderchuck's notice.

"Yes Torf, I see her too," commiserated Menderchuck. "You wish to plow her fertile fields no doubt."

"What? I don't want to be a farmer."

"You wish to mount her of course," insisted Menderchuck.

"What? She's no horse." protested Torfulson.

"Your mother was."

"Menderchuck!" exclaimed an offended Torfulson.

"Woman, come hither!" loudly declared Menderchuck.

The moderately attractive waitress stopped, turned around, and walked back over to their table.

"Is there something you need, sir?" she asked politely.

"My son wishes to mate with you," boldly declared Menderchuck. "I know he looks a bit weak and stringy, but worry not. He is of the house of Chuck. Why I myself have mounted many a woman, without a single complaint."

Torfulson flushed red with embarrassment.

"Well, good for you," replied the waitress, rolling her eyes.

"Why yes, it was good for me!" proudly exclaimed Menderchuck. "So good of you to notice, now about my son."

"I'm sorry. I'm already married."

Mortified, Torfulson slunk down in his chair.

"Oh no problem, your husband must be a lucky

man indeed," replied Menderchuck, before turning towards Torfulson and proclaiming in a voice that was loud enough for all to hear. "Sorry Torf. She's married!"

In that moment Torfulson wished that he could die, or that he at least had the ability to cast some sort of invisibility spell upon himself to escape the embarrassment of it all.

"I'm sorry," squeaked Torfulson to the waitress. "He isn't very cultured. He's a barbarian."

"It's ok, hunny," smiled the waitress, giving Torfulson a reassuring pat on the shoulder. "We get a lot of 'barbarians' in here."

Then she walked off to help another customer.

"Menderchuck, that's not how you treat a woman!" chided Torfulson in the loudest hushed tone that he could muster.

"How right you are, but I can't rightly ride my mighty steed in here, slaying the men folk, and tossing her on the back of my horse. My horse is dead. It was killed by fat archers of dubious moral fiber."

Torfulson glared at Menderchuck, but the glare was not returned. For Menderchuck had already fiercely grabbed his knife and fork and was busily assaulting his meat pie.

"Goofff," exclaimed Menderchuck's muffled food filled mouth.

"Good?" asked Torfulson.

Menderchuck nodded his head vigorously, then proceeded to shovel a fork full of mashed potatoes into his already amply full mouth. Torfulson paused for a moment, then smiled to himself. This certainly wasn't going as he had hoped, but he was glad to finally be sharing a favorite meal at his favorite restaurant with his father. And so Torfulson gingerly picked up his knife and fork and began to cut into his own meat pie.

CHAPTER 17: MEAT PIE

A few minutes later found Torfulson methodically enjoying his meat pie while he and Menderchuck sat at a table in the restaurant Immundus. As the two men ate, a lifetime of questions burned inside of Torfulson, demanding to be asked all at once. But, as Torfulson was learning, Menderchuck was not the type of man to daintily eat while he held court. He ate like a whirlwind, consuming all that was in his path.

Thus Torfulson decided to hold his questions, which burned to be asked, for just a little bit longer. Finally, Menderchuck licked his plate clean, then slammed it down upon the table.

"Ummm," began Torfulson, starring down at his mashed potatoes. "So, why did you leave us?"

"BURRRP!" belched Menderchuck. "What?"

"Wh... why did you abandon my mother and I before I was born?"

"Oh," replied Menderchuck in a suddenly despondent tone. "I didn't. Your mother left me. Maybe it was my fault. Maybe I'd mentioned one too many times how hard my own childhood had been. The life of a chief's eldest child is dangerous, difficult, and lonely. She didn't want that for you. She wanted you to have a better life, so she brought you here."

"To this restaurant?"

Menderchuck brayed with laughter, "Funny, that's a good one."

"Why didn't you come with us?" timidly inquired Torfulson.

Menderchuck squirmed awkwardly in his chair. He had once fought a rabid grizzly bear with only his trusty knife. Wrestling with emotions, he felt, was much more difficult than wrestling with that rabid bear.

"Duty," explained Menderchuck, solemnly sitting upright. "And I don't mean the kind that comes outta your butt. Admittedly, it pained me to see your mother go. Lorelei was the light of my life, a part of my world went dark when she left... but a clan chief has an obligation to his people."

Torfulson listened intently to his father's words.

"The thing is," continued Menderchuck. "A clan's chief must guide his people, from watering hole to watering hole, from village to village. He must instruct the young warriors as a teacher. He must protect the young as though they were his own children. He must see to the health and security of the tribal elders. It is his duty to protect the clan as though it were his very family, for it is. It is a bit like a father watching over his children."

"I had no father to watch over me," replied Torfulson a bit more resentfully than he had desired.

"Ha, you're lucky," chuckled Menderchuck, not

understanding Torfulson's sentiment. "My father, the chief, was always on my butt, about everything. The other kids would be out playing, and I'd be stuck inside a stuffy yurt reciting the clan's laws for hour after hour, preparing to someday become chief. Do you know what the punishment is for stealing your neighbor's chicken, wearing it as a hat, and then lying about it is?"

"No..."

"Exactly!" exploded Menderchuck. "No one does, except the clan chief, and no one should have to know! It happened once fifty years ago, and I still had to learn that useless law. And you know what young me got for pointing out how stupid that was to my father?"

"No."

"A whipping," laughed Menderchuck. "And him screaming about the sacred law. It was probably his chicken that got stolen way back when."

Slack jawed, Torfulson stared at his father, unsure of how to respond.

"Oh, and learning to fight," reminisced Menderchuck. "My father was such a slave driver. I never got to be a carefree child. I never got a day off. Day in and day out, getting beaten up by the clan's warriors as my father watched on, insisting it was for my own good. I mean, I guess in the end, it worked. I started out terrible, but eventually became one of the clan's best warriors, even finishing the Kal Bartek on the first attempt, but... I don't think it needed to be so hard."

"So..." vulnerably asked Torfulson. "You don't regret not being there where I was born?"

"You ever see a birth, kid? Ewww, gross, no thank you. And, on the plus side I got to miss out on changing diapers and losing sleep to a crying baby."

"Those are a child's formative years!" exclaimed Torfulson.

"More like annoying years," retorted Menderchuck.

A moment of silence, that was angry on Torfulson's part and oblivious on Menderchuck's, fell upon the table.

"Who's Oleg?" asked Torfulson, breaking the silence.

Menderchuck's left eyebrow arched quizzically as he stared at Torfulson.

"Mom's letter mentions him," explained Torfulson, pulling the aged letter from his shirt.

At the sight of Menderchuck's arm reaching across the table for the letter, Torfulson timidly pulled the letter back towards his chest.

"Could, could I just hold Mom's letter for a bit longer? I don't have much left from her."

"Alright," sympathetically nodded Menderchuck. "But I do want it back eventually. Maybe your mother was right about bringing you to Oppidium. Apparently, you learned to read, that's more than I can say for myself."

"I was schooled for a few years. Mom wanted it to be more, but she ran out of money, so I had to quit. It was for the better though. School was a horrible place. I was often bullied by the other children."

"Do you need me to slaughter these children for you?" inquired a deadly serious Menderchuck.

"No, no, that was many years ago," smiled Torfulson. "They aren't children any more. Anyways, bad life decisions, or the city guard have caught up with most of them by now."

Menderchuck nodded as though that was a satisfactory result.

"Oleg," began Menderchuck, remembering Torfulson's original question. "He was the head of one of the clan's richest families. He was a difficult man, but a good warrior. Your mother hoped in vain that he could take my place, and I could join her. But leading the clan was my duty, my responsibility, not his. Didn't your mother tell you anything about me?"

"No," replied Torfulson, averting his eyes from Menderchuck's. "Many times, as a child I'd ask, but she'd never talk about it. I mean, about you."

A pained, but not surprised look came over

Menderchuck's face.

"That was your mom," calmly replied Menderchuck. "She always let the past stay in the past. Speaking of Lorelei, when we first met, you mentioned she died of the plague. What happened?"

"Years ago," began Torfulson with a heavy sigh. "The black plague came to Oppidium. It spared no part of the city. The rich in the upper city and the poor in the slums died in equal measure. I saw more than a few of my friends succumb to the black death, and then it came knocking on our door..."

Torfulson struggled to maintain his composure for a moment, then continued.

"Her entire life, she had been so strong. Always working, always providing, through good times and bad. In less than a week, the plague turned the strongest person I've ever known into someone who was bedridden and helpless. She couldn't even walk. It was my turn to be strong. I fed her. I washed her. I cleaned her chamber pot and her clothes. I read her stories out of my few books. It always made her smile to hear me read to her. And then, one day, she was no more. It all happened so fast."

Torfulson held back a tear as he stared into space, "It is lonely since mom died."

A cloud of sadness descended over both men.

"Thank you for telling me, that must not be

easy," sympathetically replied Menderchuck.

Though Torfulson said not a word, the expression on his face agreed wholeheartedly with Menderchuck's words.

"So," asked Menderchuck. "What else do you want to know about me?"

"Ummmm, anything. What are your likes, your dislikes?"

For a moment, the sadness in Menderchuck's face washed away as he descended into deep thought. Then his brows furrowed, and he began to talk.

"I hate gnomes. They got these tiny little hands, and these tiny little fingers that can get most anywhere."

Menderchuck looked around the room cautiously and then continued.

"And they got real beady tiny eyes, that watch you all the time."

"Okaaay," replied a confused Torfulson. "I was thinking more like...."

Menderchuck's eyes darted wildly across the room, "Those little turds might even be in this room right now, listening in."

"I was thinking more... what is it like to be a barbarian?"

"It's freedom," wistfully replied Menderchuck. "We rode where we pleased, and raided where we pleased. Our name was feared far and wide. We lived as free men and women."

"You lived as a woman?" teased Torfulson with a sly grin upon his face.

Menderchuck rolled his eyes and continued.

"It was a tough, but good life. It could also be a violent life. Your mother didn't want that for you. Personally I couldn't imagine a better life for a young man. A little killing and raiding does a body good."

"Probably not for the person being killed," replied Torfulson.

"You sound like your mother," shrugged Menderchuck.

A well of emotions began to overflow in Torfulson as he processed it all. For as long as he could remember, he had wondered who his father was. As a child, he had wondered why his father wasn't there on birthdays and holidays. Why he had never come to see him. His train of thought had just begun to leave the station when it was abruptly derailed.

"Are you ready for the check?" asked their waitress as she approached their table.

"No, I ain't got no money," declared Menderchuck matter of factly.

Torfulson nodded to the waitress then pulled a handful of coins out of his pocket. Most of the coins were copper, but amongst them were two large rare golden ducats. He counted out enough copper coins to pay the bill, then returned the rest of the coins to his pocket.

"So, what about you Torf?" asked Menderchuck. "What'd you do? What you got cooking up?"

This was a question that Torfulson was totally unprepared for. Very seldom was anyone interested in his plans. And so Torfulson began to eagerly tell his father of his job as a milkmaid and his work on a secret plan to build a milking contraption that would change the dairy industry (and his life) for the better. Well, assuming he could get his hands on all of the necessary parts. The trickiest of which would be the blacksmith's giant bellows.

CHAPTER 18: FAMILY SECRETS

The door to the restaurant Immundus swung open, revealing the red and orange twilight hues that were now painted upon Oppidium's evening sky. Like a pair of similarly dressed brothers walking home from school, one slightly taller than the other, Torfulson and Menderchuck stepped out into the cool evening air.

"Brawwwwp," loudly burped Menderchuck. "It's almost as good coming up as it was going down."

Torfulson took little notice of his father's crude compliment. Quietly, he led his father down the dirty street, past row after row of businesses, eventually turning to merge onto the King's Highway which teemed with throngs of busy travelers.

Both men's stomachs were full, and so was Torfulson's mind. Curiosity, resentment, regret, joy, and sadness all vied for prime real estate in Torfulson's psyche. For the moment, curiosity had managed to best his opponents and snag the most coveted lake front property.

"Why?" awkwardly began Torfulson, pushing through the crowded highway. "Why if you were too busy to visit my whole life, why are you here now?"

The well fed smile on Menderchuck's face faded like an ebbing tide.

"My duty is over," explained a crest fallen

Menderchuck. "My people, our people, are no more. You and I are all that are left. The last of the Chucks."

"What happened?"

"Invaders," gravely replied Menderchuck.

Though Menderchuck walked only a few feet away from his son, his mind appeared to be thousands of miles away.

"The people of the West," darkly continued Menderchuck. "As it's always been, nothing good ever comes from there. An evil Duke named Belloch raised an army and invaded our homeland, destroying the clans. Maybe we deserved it for the sins of our fathers, but if so, then we have paid many times over. Promise me Torf, that you will never make a deal with the kingdoms of the west."

"What?" sputtered a confused Torfulson. "I hate to break it to you, but kingdoms aren't exactly knocking my door down to make deals with me. I might like a deal to buy my milking contraption plans, if you want to send them my way."

"Promise me!" erupted Menderchuck, nostrils flaring like a wild beast.

"Ok..., ok, I promise. I won't make any deals with the kingdoms of the west... though to me, I guess... those are the kingdoms of the northeast?"

"Good, good," grunted the appeased Menderchuck.

Silently, the two men continued their journey down the crowded King's Highway past the Arc De Defeat. An ancient monument erected long ago by a bygone narcissistic king who had desired to celebrate even his defeats. Its massive stone columns were covered with engraved images of his army being violently slaughtered while he (and his horse) heroically retreated at a very rapid pace.

"What sins?" asked Torfulson.

Menderchuck sighed, trying to figure out the best way to unravel the long and complicated history of his people.

"Slavery," explained Menderchuck. "An abhorrent practice. Most of the horse clans would have nothing to do with it, sadly, our clan was not one of those. For generations, villages rose up in terror as clan Chuck approached, scared of our chains."

"Menderchuck," asked Torfulson, brow furrowed in horror at his father's words. "You enslaved people?"

"No," Menderchuck gritted his teeth, holding back years of rage. "I was only a child. You know what my father did?"

"No.... what?"

"He sold my best friend, Ali, to the kingdoms of the west," grunted Menderchuck, his eyes filling with fury. "Ali didn't do anything wrong. He, like me, was just a small child. His family had no chance to out run my father's men. They were but poor villagers. Like animals, my father chained them. Like animals, he beat them, driving them before us. But that's how it was. Torf, don't ever take slaves."

"I never intended too!" croaked Torfulson, surprised by the conversation's sudden turn.

"I didn't understand then, I was too small and ignorant," sullenly brooded Menderchuck. "I just saw Ali as a new friend. A friend who made me laugh on good days and bad. He didn't care that I was the son of the chief. He, unlike most people, treated me like an equal. Little did I understand the terror and horror that my father had dragged him and his family into. Well, until we reached the West."

Torfulson's eyes took a sidelong glance in Menderchuck's direction, patiently waiting for him to continue.

"On that fateful day, with many a chained slave in tow, our clan approached the Steppes' western border," continued Menderchuck. "In yearly ritual, a mass of richly adorned westerners awaited us, eager to bid on our captives. I pleaded with my father, the chief, not to sell my best friend, but he wouldn't listen. The slaves were auctioned off one by one like cattle. I can still see Ali's face, drenched in tears, giving me one last wave as he was dragged off by some wrinkly old duchess. I too cried that day, selfishly for my loss."

"What happened to Ali?" inquired Torfulson.

"I don't know," deeply sighed Menderchuck. "I never saw him again. I never forgave my father for selling my best friend. And I'll never forget the screams, no matter how hard I try. Ali's mother screaming for her boy, as they were violently separated and sold to different people. And as I got older, that was the part that stuck with me the most. My loss was tiny compared to hers."

Silently, so as not to interrupt the story, Torfulson pointed towards a dark alleyway. The two men turned off of the King's Highway and ventured forth into the alley as Menderchuck continued his tale.

"Things were never the same between my father and I after that. We argued often. Me demanding in vain that he end the practice. He was the chief, he could have. Instead, he beat me for my insolence, calling me ungrateful for the life that slavery bought us. But it didn't stop me. As I grew, my voice grew, and I soon found many others in the clan who shared my convictions."

"You did?" asked Torfulson.

"Yes," nodded Menderchuck. "Slavery was only good for the clan's rich and powerful. They owned the chains. They made the profits. For the rest of the clan, slavery was anywhere from reprehensible to down right dangerous. If you raid a man for his gold, most will hand it over rather than die. Life is more valuable than gold. You're giving them a option, it's an honest trade... but when you come to enslave, you give them no options, and many will fight to the death rather than be captured."

"What happened next?" demanded a most curious Torfulson.

"I had to wait impatiently for change. Time moves very slowly when you're young, though it sadly makes up for that when you get older. When I reached the proper age, I completed the rites of manhood. Then I immediately challenged my father for the title of chief, as was my right under clan law. Maybe he shouldn't have forced me to spend so many years learning clan law."

A wide prideful grin spread across Menderchuck's face.

"Long story long," boldly finished Menderchuck. "I bested my father in combat and took my rightful mantle as chief, which would have been yours someday. My first act was to end the taking of slaves which was met with great joy in the clan. Well, great joy from all, but a spoiled few. And in an act of pious revenge, I made my father watch as I had the chains, that my family had used for generations to enslave, melted down to form my now legendary blade Arbjak."

"The one that's stuck in my ceiling back home?" wondered Torfulson aloud.

"Uhhh... uhhh, yeah..." awkwardly admitted Menderchuck.

As the two men strolled down the dark alley, Torfulson's mind mulled over all he had just learned.

"What about that Oleg guy?" asked Torfulson's curiosity. "Was he glad you ended slavery?"

"Ohhhh, no," scoffed Menderchuck. "He was furious. He had grown quite rich enslaving others. He raged at me, accusing me of trying to ruin him. We even came to blows. But I was the better warrior. And once I bested him, he begged for my forgiveness. And from that point on, it's been almost impossible to find a more valued warrior in all the clan than him."

Menderchuck's tone changed as though his soul was deflating, "Well... I mean Oleg was, before he was massacred... before the whole clan was massacred by Belloch's men. It's all my fault. I never should have listened to Oleg's plan, but my pride..."

"Give us your money!" interrupted a massive thug who suddenly leapt from the alley's shadows, blocking their path.

The glint of steel flickered in the dark narrow alley as two more bandits crept from the shadows, revealing large knives in their hands.

"No, I don't think I will," stubbornly replied Menderchuck even though he had no money to give.

The massive bandit, who stood a head taller than the rest, folded his arms, staring menacingly down at Menderchuck and Torfulson.

"Ummm," weakly sputtered Torfulson, slowly reaching towards his pockets. "We should probably do as they say."

Torfulson had grown up in the slums of Oppidium. He knew very well that life here was quite cheap.

"You should listen to your young friend, old timer," smugly grinned the massive thug. "Give us your money, or die."

"No," replied Menderchuck. "Give us your money."

The massive thug paused for a second, confused by the bravado of his soon to be victim.

"Ummm, no. You give. Last chance," responded the massive thug, regaining his threatening composure.

Frantically, Torfulson began to fumble in his pockets, trying to pull out his coins.

"Eat my fat weewee, you dumb turd," matter of factly declared Menderchuck.

Torfulson's eyes went wide and his mouth agape in disbelief at Menderchuck's words.

"No, no, no, you can have our money," pleaded Torfulson.

"Too late," declared the furious massive thug, advancing upon Torfulson.

Torfulson stumbled backwards, shrinking from the dangerous thug. At the exact same moment, the two knife wielding thieves began to furiously charge towards Menderchuck. While Torfulson attempted retreat, Menderchuck held his ground, standing perfectly still.

CHAPTER 19: ASSAULTED

"Die!" screamed out the first thief, lunging knife first towards Menderchuck's throat.

Like a veteran matador spinning out of the path of a raging bull's horns, Menderchuck leapt back, avoiding certain death by only fractions of an inch. Then, in one swift move, Menderchuck's right hand fiercely grabbed the thief's outstretched knife wielding wrist. At the same moment, Menderchuck raised up his left hand, throwing it palm first with the weight of his entire body into the thief's arm. *CraaaaCK*

"AGKKGGHHH!" painfully screamed out the thief, dropping the knife which clattered to the ground below.

Jagged broken bone burst out through the thief's skin while blood gushed out of the newly made hole. Limply, his broken bleeding arm swung at his side as he cowered towards the shadows.

Menderchuck had no time to celebrate though for the second knife wielding thief was now upon him.

"Ugghhfff!" grunted the second thief, running and swinging his knife at Menderchuck.

Instantly, Menderchuck dropped to his knees, watching the thief swing over him and slide past. It was then that the glint of the fallen knife caught Menderchuck's eye. Quickly, he grasped the knife from the ground, leaping to his feet and turning to face his assailant. Having stopped his overly energetic charge, the second thief now stood about ten feet away, wearing a devilish grin upon his face.

"So old timer, you got a knife too," taunted the thief, playing menacingly with his blade. "Makes us even, but do you even know how to use, ack..."

Suddenly, the thief collapsed to the ground, dead. Where his right eye had once been, there was now a knife that was stuck hilt deep in his bleeding eye socket. Menderchuck had thrown the knife with such speed and deadly accuracy that the thief hadn't seen it coming until it was much too late.

"Reminds me of old times," smiled Menderchuck to himself, before turning to see how his son's fight was going.

There he saw Torfulson, who was pinned against his will to the alley's far brick wall with his feet impotently dangling several feet above the ground. In vain, Torfulson desperately struggled against the massive thief's great left hand which held him in place.

"Ufff! OWWW! Ugh!" painfully grunted Torfulson as the thief rained down furious blows upon his body with his free hand.

Patiently, Menderchuck stood his ground, peacefully watching the beating.

"Help!" gasped Torfulson, wide eyed with fear. "Menderchuck! Help me! Please!"

At the sound of Torfulson's plea, Menderchuck darted across the alley like a wolf on the hunt, leaping upon the massive thief's back.

"GET OFF ME!" roared the furious thief, refusing to release Torfulson.

Remembering an ancient discipline technique that his grandmother had taught him long ago when he was bad child, Menderchuck grabbed the thief's ear with one hand, placing his thumb firmly into the ear's cartilage.

"OWWWW!" screamed out the thief as Menderchuck firmly twisted the thief's ear.

The furious thief released Torfulson, who fell unceremoniously to the ground with a grunt. Crashing and flailing, the thief awkwardly clawed at his back in an attempt to dislodge Menderchuck, yet stubbornly, Menderchuck clung the thief's back.

It was then that Menderchuck pulled his right leg back, kneeing the thief as hard as he could in the kidneys.

"OWWWW!!!" cried out the thief, dropping to his knees.

If the massive thief thought things were bad now, they were about to get a whole lot worse. Seizing the moment, Menderchuck rained a fury of blows down upon the back of the thug's head. With each head punch, a bone shattering crack was heard as the thief's head was driven repeated into the brick wall before him.

"Oh my gods," gasped Torfulson in horror, laying upon the ground several feet away, watching his father mercilessly assault the thief.

With one last great punch, the thug's head bounced off of the brick wall for a final time, leaving a smear of blood while his lifeless body slumped to the ground.

His work finished, Menderchuck proudly sauntered over to Torfulson, who still lay upon the ground. With an outstretched hand, he helped Torfulson to his feet. As Torfulson dusted himself off, he turned to face his father.

"Why in the world didn't you help me earlier when he was beating me?" lamented Torfulson, nursing his ribs.

"I didn't want to take the glory of your combat away from you," solemnly replied Menderchuck. "I used to hate when my father would do that to me."

"Ummm, yeah, don't worry about that in the future," sighed Torfulson, looking down at the massive dead thug who lay at his feet.

Awkwardly, furiously, Torfulson gave the corpse a swift kick before turning back towards Menderchuck.

"Wow, where were you when I was five years old and neighbor Timmy said his dad could beat up my dad?" asked Torfulson.

"Most likely, I was on the Steppes of Rannsaka.

Do you need me to beat up this Timmy's father?"

"No, no, no," laughed Torfulson. "He's like eighty years old."

Menderchuck turned deadly serious.

"I'll do it. I'm not afraid to punch the old and frail. They're the easiest to punch."

"It's getting late," smiled Torfulson, shaking his head. "Let's go home."

CHAPTER 20: OLEG

Oleg stared off into space, lost in thought.

"That'll be two gold," declared a woman's voice next to him.

"What?" asked Oleg, startled back to reality.

The woman, who lay in bed beside him, held out her hand, firmly repeating her words.

"That'll be two gold."

Just moments ago the woman had been full of energy and passion. Now she was solely focused on business.

"Of course," replied Oleg, climbing out of the ratty bed.

Slowly, he sauntered over to his clothes which were draped across a rickety chair just a few feet away. Absentmindedly, he lifted his shirt up from the chair and began dressing himself. As he did, he silently glanced around at the wallpaper that decorated the small room's walls. It was a black floral pattern on a plain red background. The wallpaper in places like this always looked the same.

Then Oleg reached down into his trousers and removed a small leather purse. This was his first action, since entering this place, which drew the woman's genuine interest. Oleg pulled two shiny gold guilders from his coin purse. Coins in hand, he walked around the foot of the bed then over to woman's side of the bed. The woman lay beneath the bed's covers, silently watching the glittering gold coins in Oleg's hands.

As Oleg approached the woman, she held her hands out for the gold coins, but Oleg ignored her. Instead, he gently placed the coins on the end table besides her, causing the woman's face to light up with a small smile. Eagerly, she turned from Oleg to face the golden coins. As she reached over to grasp the guilders, Oleg's hand shot forth with the speed of a viper.

The woman's eyes bulged with surprise, suddenly finding Oleg's large hand wrapped around her neck. Then Oleg's hand squeezed firmly. The terrified woman opened her mouth to scream, but, to her horror, no noise emerged from her throat. The veins on her face bulged, and her eyes went bloodshot as she futilely tried to gasp for air.

Desperately, she clawed at Oleg's arm scratching it and drawing blood, but it was to no avail. Oleg's hand held her neck like a vice. If she hadn't been desperately fighting for her life, she might have noticed Oleg's eyes go blank, staring off into space, once again lost in thought.

"Uhhhh..," grunted Oleg to himself. "Things sure haven't gone as I thought they would since I joined the Duke's service."

Sure, Oleg had known ahead of time that betraying his clan, having his friends and family slaughtered or enslaved, was bound to put a damper on the holidays.

There'd be no more of Grandmother Mechie's famous bread cake to ring in the New Year. Grandmother Mechie was now doomed to an eternity of slaving away in the Butarian salt mines. This thought brought a cruel smile to Oleg's face. He'd never really liked her bread cake anyways.

"Menderchuck was such a trusting fool," chuckled Oleg, remembering how easy it had been to trick Menderchuck into falling for Duke Belloch's trap. "Funny how it all started with boots."

Months, many many months before, Oleg had been alone on the plains, hunting for sport, when he had heard the cries of an injured man. In short order, Oleg had stood above the wounded man, looking down at the unexpected sight. The man, who wore clothes of a foreign cut, lay helplessly sprawled out upon the ground, his right leg broken in two.

"Help me! Help me please!" begged the wounded man. "My lord will pay you."

It was then that Oleg's greedy eyes fell upon the wounded man's boots. They were made of the finest leather, hand stitched, and polished with care. With a twisted grin, Oleg grasped the handle of his saber, carefully pulling it from its scabbard and then lifting it menacingly above the wounded man.

"No! Don't!..." screamed out the man, holding up

his hands to shield his face.

The man's screams of protest died quickly as Oleg brought his saber down, cleaving the man in two.

"Good boots," Oleg had distractedly muttered, roughly pulling the boots from the dead man's corpse.

To Oleg's surprise, as the left boot popped free of the corpse's foot, a small leather diary slipped out, falling to the ground. With curiosity, Oleg had lifted the diary from the ground and began to examine its pages. The diary's words had been a mystery to Oleg for he was not a literate man, but there was something that he did recognize, drawings. An image of the gates of Miesnatcch. A drawing of the idol of Coivus. An image of the arena at Siztok. Instantly, Oleg recognized these crude images from his clan's many raids.

"Why," Oleg had puzzled. "Would some weird stranger have a book of images from so far and wide?"

It was true, the cities were many miles apart from each other and had little in common. And so Oleg had sought the help of an old ally who could read, a slaver from the west named Collins.

"This diary looks like the work of a spy," the slaver had told him, reading through the diary's pages. "He was scouting the cities of the plains to find their weaknesses. To find out which would be good bases of operations. Judging by how deep into the plains these cities are, I would assume he is just one of a multitude of spies out there. Seems likely that an invasion is eminent."

"Who?" Oleg had asked.

"Probably Duke Belloch," the slaver had replied. "He is an ambitious man, and rumor is that he's been growing his army substantially. I think we see why."

Now if Oleg had been a good man, he could have warned his clan about the impending invasion. He could have warned all of the clans and been a hero to the plains' many horse riders, but he was not a good man.

"This Belloch," Oleg had asked. "Does he allow slavery?"

The slaver grinned and nodded yes.

"Then carry a message to the Duke from me," Oleg had boldly proclaimed. "If he makes me wealthy, if he makes me his right hand man, if he allows me first choice of slaves in raids, then I will help him capture the plains and rule them."

"And me?" the slaver had selfishly asked.

"You will be rewarded too," Oleg had promised back then, standing face to face in the wide open plains of the Steppes. "I will find you a rich paying job that is worthy of your unique skills."

Oleg blinked his eyes, returning to reality in the small room with the red and black floral wallpaper. He looked down and saw his hand still squeezing around the neck of the consort's limp lifeless body. The woman's eyes had rolled back up into her head, and her skin had turned blue.

"Stupid greedy whore," spat out Oleg, picking up the two gold guilders and placing them back into his leather coin purse. "Definitely not worth two gold."

CHAPTER 21: MONEY

"Sixty seven, sixty eight, sixty nine," anxiously mumbled Torfulson to himself as he counted the coins for a third time.

The last rays of sunset shone in through the dirty windows of Torfulson's dilapidated shack, casting long shadows upon the far wall. Forlornly, Torfulson sat upon a rickety stool in the center of the room. His eyes were transfixed on a small pile of silver coins which lay upon the table before him. Two gold ducats rested several inches away from the silver coins. The two golden coins were never counted when Torfulson was calculating his finances.

Torfulson rested his head in the palm of his hand and let out a small sigh, disturbing the room's cold silence.

"A lifetime of work, and that's all I have to show for it," lamented Torfulson. "Still, it should be enough to buy all of the parts... well... except for the giant bellows of course."

Gingerly, Torfulson lifted the two gold ducats from the table and placed them in his pocket. Then he hastily grabbed a handful of silver coins from the pile and shoved them into his pocket.

A small unpainted wood box lay on the far end of the table. He reached across the table and dragged the wood box towards the remaining pile of silver coins. In one swift motion, he swept the pile of remaining coins into the box, then shut its lid. It was only then that Torfulson noticed the last sun rays of the day streaming into his hovel.

"Where in the world is Menderchuck?" worried Torfulson aloud. "We're going to be late."

Anxiously, he stood up and began to pace around his tiny shack like a caged animal.

"Where in the hells is he? Ughhhh, I should have just told him about it. Stupid, stupid me wanting it to be a surprise. If he doesn't get here soon, it'll be too late!"

Just as Torfulson was about to head out into the slums in search of his father, the door to the shack creaked opened. There stood Menderchuck with his white bone handle knife tucked into his trousers. Determinedly, he marched into the room while keeping one hand hidden behind his back.

"Hurry! We..."

"Look Torf," interrupted Menderchuck in a serious tone. "I gotta say something."

Torfulson stood there in silent curiosity.

"You been good to me," continued Menderchuck. "Letting me stay here, and feeding me. It's more than I deserves, and don't think I'm not appreciative. So, I figured, it was my turn to pitch in."

"I'm so glad you said that," agreed Torfulson, letting out a sigh of relief. "I was thinking the

same thing, but was scared to mention...
AHHHHH!"

Torfulson let out a high pitched shriek as Menderchuck revealed his hidden hand. Menderchuck held a half dozen dead rats by their tails. With a deft swing of his arm, the rats' limp bodies flew in an arc across the room, past Torfulson, landing on the table with a squishy thud.

"What are those?!?!" screamed Torfulson, scrambling away from the table.

"Supper," replied Menderchuck, gazing at the dead rats with hungry eyes. "I found us some good and fat ones. They gonna be good eating. Mmmm, I can already hear their boiling fat crackling as they fry in a pan."

Torfulson looked down in disgust at the smashed heads and beady eyes of the dead rats, then he remembered the time. The dead rats situation would have to wait.

"Hurry and put on your good clothes, we're going out," exclaimed a frustrated Torfulson.

Menderchuck looked down at his clothes. They were the baggy hand me downs that Torfulson had given him days before. It was the only good, well, relatively good clothes that he owned. Menderchuck looked down at his clothes, then back up at Torfulson.

"Right," said Torfulson. "Let's go!"

CHAPTER 22: A NIGHT OUT

As the cloak of night wrapped around the city of Oppidium, Torfulson and Menderchuck stood in an immense line of people who were waiting outside of a great theater. Jewelry gleamed. Fine silk dresses sashayed. Elaborate gold handle walking canes tapped the cobblestone road. A multitude of men, women, elves, and even a few dwarves, all who were dressed in their finest, waited impatiently in a line that stretched several city blocks.

"Gnome!" gasped Menderchuck, rudely pushing Torfulson aside.

Fearfully, Menderchuck leapt across Torfulson, putting his son between him and the gnome. At least he thought it was a gnome.

"Oh, my mistake," declared Menderchuck, hiding behind his son and staring at the small creature who also stood in line. "It's just a very ugly child."

"Menderchuck!" erupted Torfulson, mortified by his father's outburst.

Standing at least eight stories tall and crowned with a golden dome whose gleam could be seen for miles around, the great theater dominated Oppidium's bustling entertainment district. Massive glowing letters hung upon the theater's front face high above the waiting patrons, spelling out "Visini's Opera House" in luminous words that shone brightly through the dark night.

Below the glowing letters and above the ground, a grand marquee jutted out over the packed sidewalk, bearing the words: "Tonight Only! The Bride of Hellvana! Rapalash Farewell Tour!"

Menderchuck could not read the words above him. Even if he could have, they would have meant very little to him. But to Torfulson, they meant the world.

"I can't believe we're here," eagerly exclaimed Torfulson. "It must be fate."

"We were fated to stand in a long boring line?" asked Menderchuck, eyeing the golden necklace of a nearby woman. "Man, back home these folks would have been easy pickings. Look at all the jewels that woman's wearing."

"The real jewel is Rapalash, and her farewell performance."

"Who?" absentmindedly asked Menderchuck, turning his gaze towards a golden chain which hung from a nearby rich man's pocket.

"Only the greatest opera singer of all time, Rapalash!" eagerly explained Torfulson. "You know, I saw her very first performance in this very theater, many many years ago when I was quite young. Mother took me. She loved the opera. Mom worked hard, scrimping and saving from her meager income so that she could buy us tickets for my birthday. It was a very rare treat and an absolutely magical performance. For those hours, in the darkened theater, the world washed away. There was no hunger, no cold, no

138

bullies waiting to hit me, there was just adventure and freedom. Fantastic sets, great pageantry, and elaborate costumes. A world of limitless possibilities and music. Singing that took you away."

"Yeah, Lorelei liked some dumb things," distractedly responded Menderchuck, glancing over at a woman's silver bracelet.

Torfulson's brow furrowed with anger and hurt.

"I'm just saying it's fate," grumbled Torfulson. "Mother took me to Rapalash's first performance, and I get to take you to her last..."

"How many?" interrupted a gruff voice.

To Torfulson's surprise, they had finally reached the front of the line. Hurriedly, awkwardly, he stepped up to the ticket window. There, behind the glass ticket window, he saw the owner of the gruff voice, a surly dwarf who wore an eye patch over one eye.

"Two tickets, please," replied Torfulson with a smile on his face.

"That's ten groschen," grunted the dwarf who'd had a long day.

Though ten groschen was no small amount of money to Torfulson, he still eagerly counted out ten silver coins, handing them to the grumpy dwarf. Wearily, the dwarf took the coins, dropping them into a very full coin box. Then he rolled the last two tickets off of a spool and handed them to Torfulson. As Torfulson excitedly examined the tickets in his hand, the dwarf pulled out a crude sign which read "SOLD OUT! GO AWAY!" and placed it in the window, unleashing a wave of frustrated groans and curses from the multitude that still stood in line.

"I'll give you twenty groschen for those tickets!" called out a man in a bright pink suit.

Torfulson shook his head no.

"I'll give you fifty!" offered a woman who was adorned in silk and jewels.

"I'll give you a hundred!" shouted out an elf who wore a suit of gold.

Torfulson waved off the generous offers, leading Menderchuck through the theater's gilded front doors and into its foyer.

Whereas the packed sidewalk had been abuzz with the hum of conversation, the theater's grand marbled foyer was filled with a quiet church like reverence. Their footstep's echoed off of the foyer's marble floor as the two men walked past a table, which sold opera glasses and Rapalash souvenirs, to a pair of large oak doors. There Torfulson handed their tickets to an elderly man in a vest and a small hat who silently ushered them into the theater's great performance hall.

"Woowww," gasped Menderchuck in wonder, beholding the massive theater hall around him. "I've seen entire villages that could fit in here."

The hall's immense carpeted floor was covered with row after row of chairs covered in thick red velvet. An immense stage, complete with orchestra box and bronze footlights, dominated the hall's far wall. The theater hall's other three walls were cover with rows of grand opera boxes, stacked one above another, reaching at least five stories high in all. In each grand box, a plethora of Oppidium's rich and royal sat in their finest garb, eagerly awaiting Rapalash's ultimate performance.

Above it all, there stood a great domed ceiling painted with a vibrant mural of opera stars singing to the gods. And in the center of the domed ceiling, there hung a massive crystal chandelier whose light illuminated the entire hall.

Torfulson's neck arched back as he gazed up at the chandelier. There, high above, he saw a gnome sitting in the light fixture, calmly reading a newspaper. It was the gnome's job to brighten and darken the chandelier's light as necessary. At the sight of the gnome, Torfulson held his breath and glanced over towards Menderchuck.

"Phewww," sputtered Torfulson, letting out a small sigh of relief.

Menderchuck never saw the gnome. He was much too busy staring in wonder at the elaborate plaster molding and gilding which covered the theater's walls and ensconced its opera boxes. Gently, Torfulson tapped Menderchuck on the shoulder, leading him to their seats while the excited buzz of hushed conversations rolled around them.

"This place is packed..." declared Menderchuck in awe as he sat down.

Torfulson took his seat too then glanced up at the most elaborate opera box in the theater, the King's box. It contained the only empty seats in the entire theater. The King was seldom seen at the opera. None the less, more than a few people glanced up, hoping in vain to get a peek at his royal majesty.

"Have you ever been to the opera before?" excitedly asked Torfulson.

"No," replied Menderchuck, gawking at the massive hall. "I've burned down some theaters in raids before, but nothin' near this nice or grand."

"Then you're in for a..."

"One time," interrupted Menderchuck with a chuckle. "We accidentally set fire to a theater that was in mid show. They must have been putting on some stupid farm play, or something. Cause suddenly, we see all these men dressed as chickens running out of the building on fire. Next thing you know, a pack of stray dogs starts chasing the screaming burning actors down the street. I reckon the dogs figured they'd lucked into a mess of giant baked chickens."

Torfulson gave Menderchuck a concerned glance while Menderchuck laughed heartily at his own story.

"Well," began Torfulson. "You won't see any of that tonight, at least I hope not, but you are in for an amazing treat. There's no better show than the opera. The sets, the lights, the costumes, the music, it's magical! When that singing hits you, it's like being caught up in a great wave. It can transport you anywhere."

CHAPTER 23: RAPALASH

Twenty minutes later, a packed house sat in the dark, eagerly watching the bright stage before them in anticipation of Rapalash's arrival. Like a freed soul, the symphony's melodious chords rose up from the orchestra pit, taking flight and filling the cavernous theater to the enrapturement of all those assembled. Well, all, except one.

"Zzzz, Zzzzz," snorted Menderchuck, disturbing the melodious arrangement with his brutish snoring.

"Shhh," hushed Torfulson, nudging his father.

"WHAT?!" Menderchuck's startled words reverberated throughout the theater. "Where... who... oh.... Is this play still going on?"

"SHHHH!"

"I just had the best dream, Torf," began Menderchuck, oblivious to those around him. "I was back on the Steppes riding with my clan. Man, I miss..."

"SHHHH!" rang out a chorus of angry shushes from those seated around him.

"Just be quiet," anger whispered a mortified Torfulson.

It was then, as a stage dwarf awkwardly scrambled off stage after having hastily relit a footlight, that the orchestra's instrumental changed tempo, growing in strength and intensity. Suddenly, a bright spotlight swung over to stage, revealing the opera's star.

"Rapalash!" "It's her!" "Rapalash!" Echoed out a great many hushed voices.

There she triumphantly stood, center spotlight, center left stage, Rapalash the great. She wore a great billowing violet silk dress upon her body and a silver crown upon her head. From his seat in the audience, Torfulson looked up at the great opera singer, eyes filled with that same childlike wonder that he'd had when he first saw her long ago.

Sure, she'd put on about three hundred pounds over the years. And sure, the fake Viking ship that she stood on seemed to wobble and bend under the strain of holding her immense frame, but that mattered little to Torfulson.

With a dramatic flourish, Rapalash threw her arms back and began to sing. Like the sea backdrop which covered the stage, her song rose and crashed in mighty waves throughout the theater. Like a musical tsunami; her song lifted and carried the men, the women, the elves, the dwarves, the rich, the poor, and even the gnome up in the chandelier above to a magical land far away from the problems of their regular lives. To a land free of rent, free of disease (unless it was plot convenient), free of back pain, to a land of dreams.

While several stage dwarves sweated and swore under their breath trying to push the prop Viking ship forward through pretend seas, Rapalash sang the song of Vana the Bride of Hellvana. She sang of adventure. She sang of warriors brave and true.

"From distant lands, we make our way," boldly echoed out her tremendous singing voice. "Friends and brothers, come what may."

At that cue, a dozen actors, wearing fake beards and carrying poorly made prop weapons, appeared in the ship and joined her chorus. In a harmonious crescendo, they sang of victorious raids in far away exotic lands.

Many a house wife, many a merchant, many a wealthy socialite in the audience felt the call to adventure tug on their heart strings. And so too did Torfulson, but he also felt something else, curiosity. The curiosity of introducing a loved one to an art form and wondering if they too enjoy it.

Covertly, Torfulson peeked over at Menderchuck, who sat besides him. To Torfulson's surprise, his father was captivated by the opera. Menderchuck sat on the very edge of his seat, quietly trying to sing along to the song of Vana.

"The tickets weren't cheap," thought Torfulson to himself with a smile, "but they were worth it for this moment alone."

Then Torfulson's attention was snapped back to the stage as a new song began to be sung, a song of defiance. From stage right, a background of a small village was pushed into view. At least three dozen new singers, who were dressed as armed peasants, scrambled onto stage, huddling around the faux village. Loudly, they sang a song of defiance against Vana's raiders. And so the two songs interlocked, the song of the raiders and the song of the villagers. Together they rose in crescendo. Together they dropped back down to near silence and then rose again.

In song, Rapalash, performing as the raider Queen Vana, threatened the villagers with her warriors. The villagers, in song, refused her demands. Raising a prop wood sword high above her head, Rapalash leapt to the war boat's bow which bent slightly beneath her weight.

"Come my warriors, your Queen calls. Treasure, adventure, honor and all. They call you this day. Will you come to my aid?" she called out in song.

"Yes my Queen, we raid for thee!" sang back the warriors in response.

"So, what do you think?" excitedly whispered Torfulson, turning to face his father.

To Torfulson's disappointment, Menderchuck's seat was now empty. For a moment, Torfulson's excited joy dissolved into a frustrated sadness, wearily accepting that his father had grown bored and left. But that didn't last long. As Torfulson turned back towards the stage, his eyes grew wide with surprise. There in the distance, he saw Menderchuck awkwardly climbing up onto the stage.

"Raiders strong, raiders true, your Queen calls on you. Will you come to my aid?" she sang again.

"Yes my Queen, we raid for thee!" sang the warriors in response once more.

"I'm coming!" cried out Menderchuck as he crested the stage.

In Menderchuck's enthusiasm, he ran across the stage accidentally stepping on one of the stage dwarves.

"OWWW!" painfully cried out the dwarf, letting go of the prop warship's side which then fell to the stage floor with a clatter.

With a furrowed brow, Rapalash glanced at the stage intruder for the briefest of moments, but kept on singing. First and foremost, she was a professional. Though she did not expect this kind of behavior at such a prestigious theater, she had seen her share of drunk fans rush the stage in the past.

"To raid, to raid, treasure for all," she sang as her solo reached its peak.

At that moment, the warriors raised their weapons and cheered in song. Then in a mighty rush, the warriors charged across the stage toward the defiant villagers.

"Whoooo!!!!" shouted Menderchuck, joyously joining the rushing throng of pretend warriors.

Rudely, he ripped a wooden prop sword from the hands of a nearby actor. As the warrior actors met the village actors, they began a broad pantomime of fighting. A 'warrior' would swing their blade three feet away from a 'villager,' and the villager would fall back dramatically in an over acted death as all continued to sing.

"Owwww! OHhh!!! Oooffff!!!" screamed out several of the 'villagers' in real pain.

Menderchuck slammed into the villagers, brutally smashing them left and right with his wooden sword. More than one villager would be in the middle of a line about the plight of the noble villager, when they were unceremoniously bludgeoned by Menderchuck's wooden sword. Menderchuck did not hold back.

"For the Queen, and treasure... especially treasure!" cried out Menderchuck, overtaken by the moment.

In a frenetic whirl, Menderchuck smashed his prop blade into villager after villager, knocking out more than a few who then collapsed to the stage floor like a sack of potatoes. Horrified, the warrior actors froze in place, watching their villager counter parts scream as they fled the stage. Rapalash alone continued to sing.

"Raiders strong, raiders true, your Queen calls on you. Will you come to my aid?" sang Rapalash for a third time.

But this time her verse was not met with a response from the warriors. It was met with

149

silence. It was then, and only then, that she lost her composure. She glared with daggers at Menderchuck, the man who had ruined her final performance. With a furious waddle, she flew across the stage towards him.

"Do you think this is funny?!" she screeched out at him. "I've worked my whole life to get here, and you think some dirty peasant is going to steal my moment?!"

Like a startled deer, Menderchuck stood there blankly watching the fame opera singer furiously charge him. What happened next, Menderchuck never quite remembered. But for Torfulson and the theater's great audience, they would never forget it.

"GET OFF MY STAGE!" screamed out Rapalash, swinging her mighty fist across her body.

Like a sledgehammer hitting a brick wall, Rapalash's fist collided violently with the side of Menderchuck's head. Some people will say that weak folks "hit like a girl." Those people had never seen Rapalash before. With one hit, she sent Menderchuck spiraling like a rag doll over the side of the stage and into the crowd below. For the opera patrons, the lights of the theater went on. For Menderchuck, the world went black.

CHAPTER 24: THE AFTERMATH

The opera house's massive wooden doors flew open as Menderchuck was roughly thrown from the building. His body flew through the night air, rapidly falling face first toward the cold cobblestone street below. *THUD* He landed with a hard thud and a small fart. After a brief moment, he groaned ever so slightly, pushing himself off of the ground and back up onto his feet. With slunk shoulders and a hung head, Torfulson shuffled out of the opera house in reluctant pursuit.

"Don't you ever come back, you stupid cretins! You're banned for life!" screamed out the furious theater owner.

Menderchuck and Torfulson looked back towards the voice in time to see the theater owner and his huge bouncer slam the opera house's massive doors shut. Torfulson continued to stare at the closed doors in cold silence while Menderchuck dusted himself off and walked over.

"I can see why you enjoy the opera," exclaimed a smiling Menderchuck. "You totally get caught up in it. It was quite exciting!"

Fury filled Torfulson's body.

"Which part?!?!" angrily demanded Torfulson. "Which part was exciting?!! When you ruined our once in a lifetime opportunity to see the world's greatest opera singer's final performance?! Or! Maybe! When you trampled the set screaming 'Give me your treasure, and behold my mighty loins!' or perhaps when you punched the village elder in the back of the head and he crumpled face first into the audience?!?!"

"Hmmm," pondered Menderchuck, deep in thought. "Both were good, I will admit, but I'd have to say punching that the old man was funner."

"That was a rhetorical question!" erupted Torfulson.

Menderchuck blinked vapidly. He wasn't sure where rhetoric was, or what defined their questions.

"Maybe," began Menderchuck in an attempt to fix the situation. "What you need is something to eat."

"I'm not hungry," pouted Torfulson, folding his arms.

"My treat," encouraged Menderchuck, gesturing towards a food cart which rested beneath a lit streetlamp across the dark street.

Brows furrowed, Torfulson stared at the steaming food cart. He hated to admit it, but the food smelled delicious, and he was actually quite hungry. Torfulson nodded subtly. A joyful smile spread across Menderchuck's face, who eagerly jogged across the street towards the vendor with Torfulson following close behind.

"Good Merchant," exclaimed Menderchuck. "My son would like your delicious wiener!"

"One please," shyly added Torfulson.

The vendor opened the lid to his cart. Billowing steam and the warm smell of wieners escaped into the night air.

"Hurry merchant," encouraged Menderchuck, hungrily staring at the food. "My son can't wait to taste your delicious wiener."

Torfulson slunk down in embarrassment.

"He's most hungry for your wiener," eagerly continued Menderchuck. "In fact, your hot wiener smells so good, I too would like it."

"Wieners," awkwardly corrected Torfulson.

"I know, I know," nodded Menderchuck in agreement. "He's getting his wiener ready for you Torf. Be patient. He's only one man."

The vendor grabbed a pair of metal tongs off of the side of the cart. Then he plunged them into the cart and pulled out a long steaming wiener. It glistened as the steam floated off of it. He placed it into a large fluffy bun and slathered it in mustard. He handed it to Torfulson. Then the vendor repeated the process and handed one to Menderchuck, who greedily took it.

"That'll be four copper," declared the vendor, holding out his hand.

Torfulson looked expectantly at Menderchuck.

"Whafff?" asked Menderchuck, his mouth full of breaded wiener.

Torfulson let out a long frustrated sigh.

"Of course he doesn't have any money," thought an annoyed Torfulson. "Of course he offers to treat, and I have to pay."

Torfulson reached into his pocket, pulled out a silver groschen, and placed it in the vendor's expectant hand.

"Keep the change," mumbled Torfulson.

"Thank you, sir!" replied the grateful vendor.

Menderchuck gulped down a mouthful of wiener, "Mmm, Merchant, your wiener is a bit salty, but most delicious. I do approve."

"It is good," reluctantly agreed Torfulson.

"There you go," exclaimed Menderchuck, giving Torfulson a hearty slap on the back.

This came as a great surprise to Torfulson, whose mouth was full of food.

"Goggg, ackkk, gawccckk," gurgled Torfulson, choking for a moment on his food before swallowing it.

Menderchuck gestured towards the food merchant, then proclaimed in a loud voice,

154

"Look at us! A father and son enjoying this man's wiener together! Just like you always wanted Torf!"

Mortification filled Torfulson's soul as several passersby glanced their way. He was quickly learning that having a father can be quite embarrassing at times. With a furrowed brow and an angry grunt, Torfulson grumpily stomped off into the night. Confused, Menderchuck continued to chew his hot wiener, watching his son storm off.

"This parenting thing is difficult," confided Menderchuck to the nearby merchant. "I try to get into the things my son likes, like the opera, but it just seems to make him mad."

"I get it," sympathetically nodded the merchant. "It can be hard, and frustrating, like nothing you do even matters. I, myself, have five amazing daughters, three are teens. It may not seem like they want you around, but they do. The important thing is just to make the effort."

"Is that what you do?" timidly inquired Menderchuck.

"Hells no," replied the merchant. "Are you kidding me? Five daughters and my wife, in one house. They are all constantly fighting. Rawwrrrr, there's never any peace. That's why I'm out here working all hours of the night, praying to the gods to kill me. I make more money out here, and I can avoid that total poop show back at home."

In the middle of the night, under a star filled sky, beneath the light of a lamppost, Menderchuck the barbarian and the wiener merchant stood in a brief moment of silence.

"Well," began Menderchuck, breaking the silence. "One more wiener please."

"Coming up," replied the merchant with a smile.

The vendor once again repeated the ritual of food preparation and handed Menderchuck a bun filled wiener.

"That'll be two copper," stated the vendor.

Menderchuck froze. He didn't have any money. The vendor stared at him for an awkward minute, then Menderchuck shoved the whole wiener into his mouth and ran off.

"Someone stop that man!" shouted out the vendor. "He's stolen my wiener!"

CHAPTER 25: HOT NIGHT

The Bayan river flowed lazily through the heart of Oppidium, filling the city's hot night air with a smothering blanket of humidity.

clack *clack* *clack*

"Uggghhh," groaned Menderchuck as he was awakened by the sound of the rickety outhouse door.

Sweat trickling down his body, Menderchuck sat up, trying to get his bearings. Groggily, he looked around the small dark bedroom. Moonlight drifted in through the room's lone window. Menderchuck reached down and felt the crude straw bed beneath him.

"Uhhhggg, I hate this bed. It's too soft," grumbled Menderchuck. "This room is too stuffy, too confining, too stupid! I miss sleeping on the firm ground of the plains, beneath the stars, where you're wild and free. I miss falling asleep to the sounds of the fire crackling and the animals of the night, as man was meant to. I don't know how they live like this, in these horrid cages..."

Menderchuck punched the bed in frustration, but was then hit with a tinge of guilt. The small bedroom was the only bedroom in Torfulson's shack, and he had generously given it to Menderchuck to use.

clack *clack* *clack* Went the outhouse door

again. From bed, Menderchuck glanced out through the window. There he saw Mrs. Watterson limping out of the nearby outhouse.

"She's already been in there four times tonight!" angrily thought Menderchuck. "She must have eaten some of her husband's cooking. By the gods, I want to punch her in her giant stupid head. Quit opening and closing that stupid door! How much poo can one woman have in her stupid body?!"

Now normally, Menderchuck was very fond of Mrs. Watterson. She was a kind elderly woman who enjoyed a saucy joke. They were kindred spirits in that, but tonight Menderchuck was not coping well with the oppressive humidity.

Menderchuck's home, the plains of Rannsaka, were a dry place, unlike the miserable sweltering humidity of Oppidium's night. The kind of humidity that made you hate the entire world and everyone and everything in it. The kind of humidity that would make you snap at someone for breathing too loudly, eating too loudly, or talking too much.

"Ugggh!" grunted Menderchuck, frustratedly tugging on his beard. "I want this off! Too hot... Is this why so many of this town's titty babies are clean shaven?"

Back home on the Steppes of Rannsaka, such a thought would have been tantamount to sacrilege. In the horse clans, a beard had been a stately symbol of manhood. The men of the clan took great pride and vanity in their beards,

158

priming and trimming them often. In fact, for some offenses to the clan, you could be shaved clean in shameful punishment for all to witness.

"Batu," mumbled Menderchuck to himself, remembering his old uncle.

Many years ago, Uncle Batu had had the longest most majestic beard in the entire clan. It flowed like a mighty river from his face all the way down to his feet. Menderchuck chuckled lightly, shaking his head as he thought of the past.

"Old Batu was always bragging that his manhood was as long as his beard. Well, until that day..."

Batu had stood tall in the wide open grassy plains of Rannsaka with a small audience huddled around him. Once again, he bragged loudly of his beard's magnificence to the great embarrassment of his children.

"Behold the beard of GLORY! My beard is the greatest beard in all the clan!" Batu had boasted proudly to all who would listen. "Your beards are insignificant compared to mine! Feel the beard shame in your souls!"

The children's embarrassment soon turned to laughter as one of the clan's many goats walked up and began to nibble on the end of Batu's beard.

"Witness this, all!" Batu had proudly declared, throwing his arms high into the air. "Even this goat knows that my beard is better than all of yours. For I ammmmmmmmmmmm, AHHHHHHH!!!!!"

The look of pride fled in an instance from Batu's face and was replaced with the visage of fear. Batu jerked forward, face first, then crashed to the ground. In an instant, his body was careening wildly through the plain's tall grass, dragged forward by the galloping goat who held Batu's beard firmly in its teeth.

The goat had dragged the screaming Batu over a hundred yards, beard first, before it finally released the beard and let him go. It had taken Batu a few moments to regain his composure and shakily climb back up to his feet. The clan had roared with laughter, seeing the now distant Batu covered face, body, and beard in mud. In the moment, Batu had been filled with fury and mortification, but that would soon pass. In the years to come, he would often joyfully regale others with the tale of his beard and the goat.

Sitting alone in the Torfulson's bedroom on a miserable sweltering night, Menderchuck smiled to himself, thinking about his silly uncle. But the smile only lasted a moment. As one ages, even happy memories can be tinged with sadness. Especially when we think about those people and places that we once loved, who are now gone forever.

"I miss home. I miss the plains," wistfully sighed Menderchuck.

Menderchuck looked at the dark cramped bedroom around him and had a thought that filled him with a desolate sadness.

"I guess this is my home now..."

clack *clack* *clack* Went the outhouse door. Mrs. Watterson was making her fifth visit for the night.

CHAPTER 26:
A HARD DAY'S WORK

squish *plop* *squish* *plop* Trudged Torfulson's weary feet, plowing through the muddy bog of a street which ran through the decaying slums that he called home. A brief late afternoon rain storm had transformed the dusty streets into a muddy wonderland to the joyous delight of the boisterous dirty street urchins who laughed and played in its soiled mud. For Torfulson though, navigating the difficult sticky streets which stubbornly clung to his feet, it was a fitting and unwelcome end to a long hard day's work.

"I wish I still lived alone," sighed Torfulson, coming to a halt and pausing for a moment outside of his hovel.

Regret instantly seeped into Torfulson's soul.

"I... I mean," backtracked Torfulson. "I'm glad Menderchuck lives here too, and I wouldn't want him to leave... I just wish I had a day alone."

Reluctantly, Torfulson threw his work bag over his shoulder and entered his home in search of some peace and quiet. His search was in vain for no sooner had he stepped into his home's small main room when he heard his father's booming voice.

"Owww! You son of a butt!" Menderchuck's voice rang out from the adjacent bedroom.

"Ugh..." grunted Torfulson, tossing his work bag onto the far edge of the main room's old wooden table.

Wearily, Torfulson bent down and began a brief struggle to free his muddy shoes from his feet. Once free, he sauntered over towards the room's crooked stone fireplace, setting his muddy shoes on its hearth to dry. Then he plopped down upon one of the three legged stools which rested around the old table.

"Urrrrr..." mumbled Torfulson, running his frustrated hands through his hair.

It was then that he glanced around the small room. His eyes fell upon the large rolled up piece of paper which rested beside the broken milking contraption in the room's far corner. Through the wear and tear, through the frustration and pain, a weak smiled crept across Torfulson's face. Gingerly, he climbed to his feet and crossed the room.

"Hello old friend," grinned Torfulson, his spirits lifting slightly as he lifted the great rolled paper from the floor.

Cautiously, he carried the paper to the center of the room, placing it carefully upon the table. Though Torfulson had perused his plans for a better milking contraption a thousand times; they, and the hope of a brighter future that they represented, always brought a smile to his face. Reverently, like a priest unrolling sacred texts, Torfulson began to unroll the great sheet of paper.

"ARRRR!" roared out Torfulson in frustration.

For as he unrolled the great sheet of paper, a multitude of wood shavings were released from the formerly pristine paper's hold.

"Menderchuck!" furiously erupted Torfulson.

"You rang?" smiled Menderchuck, strolling into the doorway that separated the two rooms.

"What did you do to my plans?! There's wood shavings everywhere! And what's this? Are these tea stains?!!!"

The smiled drained from Menderchuck's face.

"I'm sorry about the mess," solemnly apologized the barbarian as he approached his son. "I... I made you this."

Menderchuck held out his left hand, revealing a crumpled bloody handkerchief.

"My good handkerchief?" lamented Torfulson with furrowed brows.

"No... I mean yes," stumbled Menderchuck. "I kinda bled on it. The present, though, is in the handkerchief. Take it. Take it."

"Ewwww," grumbled Torfulson, taking the wet bloody handkerchief in hand.

With a grimace on his face, Torfulson pulled back the handkerchief's edge, revealing a wooden gear.

"I carved it myself," proudly grinned Menderchuck. "Though I might have carved a bit of myself too."

Torfulson stared quizzically at the wooden gear which rested in his hand.

"How?..." incredulously asked Torfulson. "How did you know how to make a gear?"

"It wasn't that hard," explained Menderchuck, pointing towards Torfulson's plans. "See, it's right there in your diagram. And you drew it next to a coin picture, so I figured that was the scale to use, and it's not like it's the first time I've seen a gear."

"When have you ever seen a gear?" demanded a perplexed Torfulson.

"Years ago we raided this miller out in Sharga. He had this great windmill. I could have spent all day in there, just watching the gears turn as the millstone.... ummm... milled."

Silently, Torfulson stared in surprise at the mental image of his father studying gears in motion.

"Oh, and then we started smashing things in it," laughed Menderchuck. "The miller was not happy with that, yelling at us to stop. I put a watermelon in the gears. Boom! It exploded everywhere. It was great! Oleg put a chicken in the gears. I didn't really approve of that so much. It exploded in a shower of feathers and blood. And then Pavel ruined it all. He put a large stone

165

in the works, which broke the gears, breaking the windmill. Man was the miller mad."

Mouth slightly agape, Torfulson stood there quietly trying to process it all.

"So... ummm.." awkwardly continued Menderchuck. "I remembered that when we went to that restaurant, you mentioned working on that milking contraption, and I thought I'd help. So I whittled you that gear."

With his free hand, Torfulson lifted the wooden gear from the bloody handkerchief and turned it over in his hand.

"This, this looks like it'll work," declared Torfulson, studiously examining the gear. "The symmetry appears to be well within working limits. It's well carved. Can, can you make anything else from my plans?"

Menderchuck looked down at the mass of notes and drawings which covered the large sheet of paper.

"Well," admitted Menderchuck, shyly kicking the floor with a foot. "I can't read any of them notes, but the stuff you drew I can probably carve, so long as you get me the wood."

"I can explain the notes as we come to them," eagerly responded Torfulson with a hopeful smile upon his face.

"Well then, Torf," nodded Menderchuck. "I'm willing to give it a try."

CHAPTER 27:
BUT DOES IT BLOW?

As the weeks went by, Torfulson spent his ever dwindling savings on the raw materials that he needed for the new and improved milking contraption. Each night after a hard day's work, he would rush from the dairy farm to some local merchant or other to purchase new bits of metal and wood. Then he would head home for a late night of crafting and assembly. There he would find an unexpected teacher in Menderchuck.

Under his father's tutelage; Torfulson, using the whittling knife that he had purchased as a child long ago, was quickly learning how to carve serviceable gears and lynchpins.

"You want to cut with the grain," Menderchuck had explained. "Yeah, you're getting it. Looks good. Just keep at it."

A long desired pride filled Torfulson's soul as a small smile spread across his face at the sound of his father's encouraging words.

As Torfulson's money dwindled, the pace of work hastened. Each morning before heading to work on the dairy farm, Torfulson would give Menderchuck instructions on what needed to be done that day on the milking contraption. And each night when Torfulson returned from work, he would check Menderchuck's progress and make any needed adjustments.

"Wow," Torfulson had gratefully thought to

himself. "What I lose in wages paying for Menderchuck's food is more than made up by his work on the contraption, and... it's nice having him here."

And so it came to be one day that most of the contraption's pieces were finished. All, that is, except the most expensive and difficult part to get.

The light of a lone bent candle flickered and danced off of the interior wall's of Torfulson's humble shack, keeping the night's darkness at bay. Near the center of the room, beside the room's rickety table, sat Menderchuck upon a wobbly stool. In one hand he held a fist size block of wood, and in the other he held his white bone handle knife.

While Menderchuck calmly shaved slices of wood from the block, Torfulson paced maniacally around the small room. In both hands, Torfulson carried a large piece of paper which rapidly flapped and flailed around as his arms wildly gestured about. It was the diagram of the milking contraption that he had drawn many weeks before.

"What was I thinking when I drew this?! Why did I ever design this around the giant bellows?!" exclaimed Torfulson out loud in self flagellation.

Menderchuck said not a word. Instead, he tried to focus on the wooden gear that he was attempting to carve. Menderchuck was not a fan of Torfulson's pacing. Out on the plains, such behavior was discouraged as it spooked the horses. And in the confined space of the hovel, it annoyed Menderchuck all the more. Plus he knew the answer to Torfulson's rhetorical question for he had heard it often before.

"There was no other way to make it work," sighed Torfulson, answering his own question. "The only way the milking contraption will work is if we can generate an immense sucking force."

In the room's far corner, upon the floor, there lay the remains of several destroyed bellows of normal size. Torfulson had attempted to connect them together to replicate the sucking power of a bigger bellows to no success. The pressure had merely popped the regular sized bellows, as though they had been cheap balloons.

thud *thud* *thud*

The sounds of anxious footsteps ran circles around Menderchuck while Torfulson continued to annoyingly pace throughout the cramped room.

"Only the blacksmith's bellows have the sufficient structural integrity needed to make the machine work!"

"Struncktuel what?" asked a very confused Menderchuck, but Torfulson paid him no mind.

"I can't afford to buy the bellows," ranted Torfulson. "Did you know the blacksmith paid four thousand gold guilders to have them custom made for him? If I worked for a hundred years at Jennix's farm, I still wouldn't have that much money! I tried to rent the bellows from him, but he refused. What a luddite! He has no vision! He doesn't want to risk his precious bellows on such a important project."

"I wonder why," sarcastically mumbled Menderchuck, glancing over at the graveyard of destroyed bellows.

"Exactly! Me too," exclaimed Torfulson, not quite getting Menderchuck's sarcasm. "How do we get giant bellows that we can't afford to buy, or rent, and that we don't have the ability to make ourselves?"

Torfulson's pacing came to an abrupt stop. His head hung low, and his shoulders slunk in defeat. The loud thud's of his anxious feet were replaced by the quiet calm sounds of Menderchuck's knife whittling wood.

"We could steal it," calmly suggested Menderchuck.

"No, no. The blacksmith is a good man. He doesn't deserve that."

"You could give up," proposed Menderchuck.

"No! We've come so far," protested Torfulson. "All we need is this last part."

"We could steal it," suggested Menderchuck again.

Torfulson stared over at Menderchuck with the furrowed brows of disappointment. Gently,

Menderchuck placed the proto wooden gear and his knife down upon the table.

"Tell you what, Torf. I think I know someone who can solve our problem."

"Really?" skeptically asked Torfulson.

"No promises, but I saw this place a while back as I was running away from the wiener man."

"Whaaaa?" wondered Torfulson.

"Come on," gently encouraged Menderchuck, rising to his feet. "Follow me."

CHAPTER 28: EYE SEE

A multitude of stars twinkled and shone high above the crowded metropolis of Oppidium, almost as though the gods themselves had punctured a million pinpricks into the black night sky. Far below, two men scurried down one city street and then up another. At times, the lead man seemed lost, often pausing at intersections then back tracking from whence they'd came.

"It's ok, if you can't find it," assured Torfulson, before he was once again abruptly pulled in another direction.

"No, no, no," dissented Menderchuck. "I know it's around here somewhere. Yes, this way! That night, there was a duck right there, who tried to fight me, stupid uppity duck. I got the best of him though."

Menderchuck grabbed Torfulson and pulled him excitedly down an alley and then onto a main road. They walked half a block further before Menderchuck stopped suddenly, turning towards a crooked one story building with a smile upon his face.

"Ta da!" exclaimed Menderchuck. "Here we'll find the answers to our many questions."

The building was squat and bent, as though some giant had sat on it long ago. Its outer walls were covered by faded pink paint which was peeling off in small strips. The front right of the building was dominated by a dirty stained glass window that depicted the image of an open hand. And in the center of the hand's palm, was the image of an all seeing eye. Set in the window below the hand, cut in purple glass, was the name 'Lady Ma'Lam.'

A weathered green door stood up a small flight of stairs to the left of the stained glass window. Set in the door about chin high, covered in cryptic runes and arcane symbols, was a cast iron knocker which was shaped like a man's fist.

"Pretty good, huh?" victoriously smiled Menderchuck, pointing towards the small building.

Torfulson sighed as hope drained from his body. He tried to think of a kind and polite way to tell his father that the fortune tellers of Oppidium are scam artists who preyed on moronic rubes from the country.

"Fortune tellers are scam artists that prey on moronic rubes from the country," flatly announced Torfulson. "Hmmm, that wasn't exactly how I meant it to come out."

Torfulson's words of doubt mattered little to Menderchuck, who bounced up and down excitedly.

"No, no, this is real! So, should I knock on the door, or should you?"

"I going home," declared a defeated Torfulson.

"No, you're not. We've got answers to find."

Eagerly, Menderchuck grabbed Torfulson with one hand and pulled him up the stairs towards the green door. Then, with his free hand, he grabbed the iron door knocker and knocked three times.

"Ohhhh," exclaimed Menderchuck. "The door knocker is cold. It must be connected to the spirit realm."

"Or it's just been outside on a cool night," mumbled Torfulson, crossing his arms.

With a small creak, the green door slowly swung open, revealing a middle aged woman. She wore a purple dress and a silver belt with silver tassels. Her white blouse was unceremoniously stained with the remains of some past meal. Her hair was long and dark, and she wore a small round violet hat upon her head.

"Whaaat?" gruffly demanded the lady.

"We..." began Menderchuck before being cut off.

"This ain't no brothel. So if you want that, scram," declared the woman, looking Menderchuck up and down. "Well, maybe I'd make an exception in your case."

"Are you a fortune teller?" excitedly asked Menderchuck.

"Yup," grumbled the woman. "I'm the one and only, Lady Ma'Lam. You want your fortune read, or something?"

"See!" triumphantly erupted Menderchuck to Torfulson. "She already predicted why we're here! I told you it's real! She'll have the answers!"

Lady Ma'Lam rolled her eyes and gestured for the two men to enter. Before Torfulson could protest once again, Menderchuck grabbed his son by the arm, pulling him into the small building.

"Follow me," commanded the medium, leading the two men down a dark narrow corridor and into her parlor.

A flickering light danced off of the parlor's faded walls, cast by an anemic fire which stubbornly clung to life in the room's crooked fireplace. As Torfulson's curious gaze turned toward the fireplace, he discovered a great assortment of various ceramic cat shaped figurines that were crammed together, covering every spare inch of the fireplace's mantel. In fact, the entire room was filled with such curios. Numerous shelves, which lined the room's walls, were littered with a host of cat shaped idols.

"Ugh," quietly grumbled Torfulson, his nostrils flaring at the overwhelming smell of incense and wet cat which hung heavily in the air.

The parlor's windows were covered by beaded curtains, and its walls were covered by arcane symbols. In the center of the room, there stood a round table with a green velvet table cloth upon it. Two spherical objects lay upon the table covered by a small purple cloth.

Lady Ma'Lam took a seat at the table in the middle of the room, then beckoned the two men to do the same. As Menderchuck and Torfulson took their seats besides the table, Lady Ma'Lam lifted up the small purple cloth, revealing a pair of identical crystal balls.

"Nice balls," dryly stated Torfulson.

"Funny, kid," sardonically replied the woman. "That's the first time I've heard that one."

It clearly was not the first time that she had heard that one. Then the woman began to mutter dark words under her breath, waving her hands above the crystal balls.

"Whadda ya see? Whadda ya see?" impatiently badgered Menderchuck.

The woman's voice became mysteriously deep and slow as she waved her hands slowly above the balls, "You come from far away."

"I do!"

"Anyone could guess that by his accent," dismissively scoffed Torfulson, rolling his eyes.

Lady Ma'Lam, the fortune teller, furrowed her brow. Maybe it was because she was a woman, maybe it was because she was a fortune teller; but either way she was used to unsolicited idiots constantly trying to "correct" her, and it did not please her.

Lady Ma'Lam's voice became dark and gritty as

she waved her hands once again, "You work with horses."

"I do!" exclaimed Menderchuck, his eyes lighting up. "How did you know that?!"

"You smell of horses," sullenly declared Torfulson, letting out a long sigh. "I don't know why, but even after all this time living with me, you still smell of horses. Anyone can tell that from a mile away."

"I bathe in the horse trough across the street," proudly beamed Menderchuck while Torfulson looked on with disgust. "Smells like home!"

"Let's go, this is all just a stupid scam," angrily demanded Torfulson.

"Fine," exclaimed Lady Ma'lam in a huff, dropping her mysterious gravely voice while staring straight into Torfulson's eyes. "Let's just take all of the fun and mystery out of it, why don't we? Sure, I sacrificed my youth studying the arcane arts. Sorry brother, I can't come to your birthday party this year, cause I have to spend the night in a abandoned graveyard talking to a boring incontinent ghost, so that I may learn to commune with the spirit world to better guide humanity, but who gives a rat's poop about that?! Kiddie here is in a rush."

Torfulson squirmed awkwardly in his chair.

"This man is your father," continued Lady Ma'lam, pointing towards Menderchuck. "He is from the Steppes of Rannsaka. He is

Menderchuck the Great and Terrible. And in five seconds he's going to let out a rancid fart, which is going to make me regret ever having let the two of you into my parlor."

The weak crackling sounds of the anemic fire filled the new found awkward silence while Torfulson counted quietly to himself. "One, two, three, four, five."

"Times up," declared a self righteous Torfulson. "Looks like you..."

rippppp Menderchuck let out a large, long, nasty fart. It sounded like and felt like it was going to go on forever.

"She's right again!" joyously exclaimed Menderchuck.

"Oh gods," coughed Torfulson. "Someone open a window."

Lady Ma'Lam covered her nose, then leapt up and rushed towards a nearby window. It was draped with a beaded curtain and surrounded by incense burners. She knocked over several unlit burners, trying desperately to open the window.

At first, to her great relief, the window began to lift up. But then, to her horror, the window stopped when it got caught on the beaded curtain. She tried to push the window back down, to lift it up again, but to no avail. The beads were firmly wedged into the window's path, leaving it stuck mostly shut.

"Oh screw it!" she cried out.

The exasperated fortune teller grabbed a small cat idol from a nearby shelf and hurled it through the window. The window's glass shattered outward as the cat idol burst through it and into the street beyond. All three inhabitants of the room gasped as one, desperately breathing in the much needed fresh air. Well, at least as fresh as the air of Oppidium ever gets.

Lady Ma'Lam then smoothed down her dress, attempting to regain her composure and act as though nothing had happened. No one wants to see a fortune teller who doesn't seem to be in control of things.

"Do me, do me, do my fortune!" excitedly requested Torfulson.

"I thought you didn't believe in this," incredulously huffed Lady Ma'Lam.

"You've change my mind."

Slowly, Lady Ma'Lam walked back towards the table and sat back down, then she began to wave her hands methodically above the crystal balls.

"I see..." she began.

"Yes?" eagerly wondered Torfulson.

"I see..."

"Yes, yes?!"

"I see great pain in your immediate future," declared Lady Ma'Lam in a deep echoing voice.

"That's a pretty poop fortune," sighed Torfulson aloud.

In a flash, Lady Ma'Lam's hand darted across the table and slapped Torfulson hard in the face.

"Owwww!" cried out Torfulson.

"The prophecy, it is complete!" shouted an excited Menderchuck.

"No it isn't, she just hit me!" cried out the wounded Torfulson, but Menderchuck ignored him.

"Marvelous Lady Ma'Lam," declared Menderchuck. "Tell me more of my future."

Lady Ma'Lam glanced once again at her crystal balls, peering deep into their depths.

After a moment, she looked up and proclaimed, "I see more pain in your son's future."

Instantly, she reached her right hand out to slap Torfulson, but this time Torfulson was ready. He blocked her hand with his and smirked.

"What now, witch?" smugly asked Torfulson.

With the speed of a viper, Lady Ma'Lam reached across the table and slapped him hard with her left hand, taking him totally by surprise.

"Owww!!!"

"She's right again!" shouted Menderchuck. "She's the greatest fortune teller in all the land!"

Torfulson nursed his red face, staring at the fortune teller.

Lady Ma'Lam stared back and spoke, "I have one last fortune for you."

"What is it?! What is it?!" excitedly asked Menderchuck.

"Your son is going to leave here poorer than when he entered," replied Lady Ma'Lam. "Now that'll be five copper coins."

Lady Ma'Lam held out her hand. Reluctantly Torfulson began to dig around in his increasingly bare pockets for some copper coins. He pulled out his last five copper coins and placed them in the fortune teller's hand. Then Lady Ma'Lam guided the two men towards the door and shut it briskly behind them.

In the cool night air, below the twinkling evening stars, the two men stood on the street outside of Lady Ma'Lam's building. Torfulson frowned and looked down towards the dirt street beneath his feet.

Menderchuck smiled and looked up towards the starry heavens, "That was amazing! I got to meet Lady Ma'Lam."

"Did you even know who she was before today?"

"Nope, but she was amazing," joyously replied Menderchuck.

"We didn't get any of the answers we need!" cried out Torfulson, kicking a rock on the ground beside him. "What good was paying for a fart prediction?! Sigh... How are we going to get the giant bellows to finish the milking contraption?"

"Like I said before, we could steal the giant bellows."

Standing despondently in the middle of the desolate road, the gears of Torfulson's mind began to whirl. He had tried alternatives and they had failed. Small and weak, Torfulson's voice cut through the night air.

"I... don't know what to do. I'm exhausted with being poor and hopeless. This is my one shot at a better life. I've poured everything into this milking contraption. My life savings, all our work. We've tried everything else I can think of. It's either give up and flush it all down the drain... or... I guess we could steal it."

"That's my boy!" shouted Menderchuck, giving Torfulson an encouraging slap on the back.

"Yeah, yeah, we can steal it," repeated Torfulson, starting to gain confidence. "We probably only need to prove that the device works. Once the blacksmith sees it works, he'll surely understand. And once we've made enough money from the milking contraption, we'll pay the blacksmith back for the giant bellows. No, wait, even better, we'll make him an equal partner with us. We'll all be rich. Then he'll be able to buy a thousand new giant bellows, if he desires!"

"Sure, whatever you want, kid," agreed Menderchuck.

"Yeah, let's do it!" boldly exclaimed Torfulson. "Let's steal the blacksmith's giant bellows... but one rule."

"What's that?" wondered Menderchuck.

"No killing."

"Awwww, not even a little killing?" whimpered a disappointed Menderchuck.

"No, no killing at all."

"Alright," shrugged Menderchuck in agreement.

CHAPTER 29: STEALING

A lonely full moon hung high in the starry night sky, shining its light over the sleepy metropolis of Oppidium while the chirping of crickets carried on the evening air. Even the King's Highway was vacant at this hour. Its empty streets ran through the deserted market square, whose many colored stalls were closed up for the night.

Torfulson and Menderchuck stood hidden in the shadows of a side street off of the west side of the King's Highway. Both of their eyes were singularly fixated on the same object, the blacksmith's giant bellows. Across the King's Highway, there stood the blacksmith's open air shop. It was abandoned, closed for the night. Close to the center of the shop, near the forge, there stood the giant bellows.

They were the largest bellows not only in Oppidium, but in the entire kingdom. They were larger than a man and blew much harder. It was said that it had taken the skins of six fully grown cows to assemble enough leather for their construction. The giant bellows rested on a large wooden frame that held up their immense weight. No single man could carry these bellows by hand, nor any married man. The blacksmith had paid a prince's ransom for them, but they had been well worth it.

"Master craftsmanship," whispered Torfulson, his eyes transfixed upon the distant giant bellows. "But we need to come up with a plan on how to sneak across the highway unseen."

The gears in Torfulson's mind began to furiously whirl, pondering, analyzing, and calculating the best way to cross the quiet highway in secret.

"Perhaps," conspiratorially whispered Torfulson. "If we hide in the lee of that donkey cart, then dart behind that stall, then crawl across the ground on our bellies behind the taffy makers, well, we'd almost be there. What do you think?"

Torfulson's question was met with silence.

"Menderchuck? Menderchuck... where are you?..."

Torfulson's eyes darted wildly around the dark side street in search of his father, but he was nowhere to be seen. Frantically, Torfulson turned from the dark street and gazed again towards the King's Highway. Suddenly, his eyes grew wide with surprise at the sight of Menderchuck strutting nonchalantly across the King's Highway towards the blacksmith's shop.

clank *clank* *clank*

It was at that exact moment that Torfulson heard the worrisome sounds of heavy footsteps walking directly toward Menderchuck.

"Please don't be a guard, please don't be a guard," quietly prayed Torfulson, ducking deeper into the shadows.

It seemed that the gods were much too busy tonight to answer Torfulson's prayers. To his dismay, the reflection of moonlight off of a steel

185

helmet stepped into view. And beneath the helmet, wearing a shiny metal breast plate upon his body and a razor sharp sword upon his belt, was a city guard.

Oppidium's city guards were the answer to the age old question: "What would happen if we took a bunch of ignorant poorly trained individuals, then armed them and gave them superiority complexes with little oversight?"

"Menderchuck!" whispered Torfulson as loudly as he dared. "Look out, guard!"

But his voice was much too quiet, and his father was much too far away. Menderchuck continued to boldly strut across the street towards the blacksmith's shop while the guard continued to walk in his direction. In very short order, the guard's path crossed that of Menderchuck's.

"Evening," greeted Menderchuck, nodding politely at the guard.

"Evening," grunted the guard who then continued down the King's Highway in patrol.

Menderchuck calmly crossed the King's Highway and walked into the blacksmith's open air shop.

"Alright," began Menderchuck, eagerly clapping his hands together. "Let's do this.... Torf?"

Confused, Menderchuck glanced about the shop, abruptly realizing that he was all alone. Then he gazed back across the highway where he spotted

186

Torfulson, who still lay in hiding. Shaking his head, Menderchuck gestured impatiently for Torfulson to follow.

Cautiously, Torfulson stepped out of the alley's shadows and into the street, revealing a shiny purple mask upon his face. Then he awkwardly jogged across the street to Menderchuck.

"What in the world are you wearing?" incredulously whispered Menderchuck.

"It's a mask, so they can't identify me."

"It's got shiny purple sequins all over it. You stand out like a sore thumb!" castigated Menderchuck.

"It's the only one I have," argued Torfulson. "And, unlike you, no one will recognize me!"

"Maybe if you're going to a fancy ball," grumble whispered an annoyed Menderchuck. "But does it look like there are any fancy balls here in the blacksmith's shop in the middle of the night?"

"No," sulked Torfulson.

"The key to doing something illegal, is to act like you're supposed to be doing it," instructed Menderchuck. "Stay calm, act normal. If you do that, no one will ever question you."

"Meooow."

A fluffy grey cat stood behind them meowing for attention. Instantly, Menderchuck spun around, locking eyes with the cat.

"Look out!" screamed out Menderchuck. "It's an alarm cat!"

Suddenly, Menderchuck ran full force towards the cat. With a swift kick, he punted the cat over a nearby fence.

"Raaaeeeoooowww," screeched the cat as it flew through the air.

In a flash, a light went on in the blacksmith's home.

"Crap Torf!" exclaimed Menderchuck. "I think your shiny mask woke them up! Grab the bellows, and blow!"

Frantically, awkwardly, the two men ran to the giant bellows. It stood chest high and rested on a large four wheeled wooden frame. Torfulson tried desperately to push the bellows with all his might, but they wouldn't budge. While Torfulson repeatedly threw his body weight into the great wooden frame in vain, Menderchuck glanced down towards the frame's large wooden wheels. There he saw a set of foot brakes which locked the frame's wheels in place.

Hastily, Menderchuck stomped down upon the foot brakes, releasing the wheels. Instantly, Torfulson and the bellows lurched forward. As they did, Torfulson's head snapped back, smacking face first into some low hanging blacksmithing tools.

"OWWW!" bellowed Torfulson as his mask caught on a dangling pair of metal tongs and was roughly torn from his face.

SLAM

Behind them, the door to the blacksmith's home burst open, hitting the side of the house. Out stepped the furious blacksmith, crossbow in his hand.

"Get your hands off my bellows, you thieves!" furiously screamed out the blacksmith.

Menderchuck and Torfulson leaned into the great wood frame, desperately pushing it with all their might.

creak *creak* *creAK* *CREAK* *CREAK*

The creaking sounds of the frame's wheels grew louder and louder as they began to turn, driving the great bellows quicker and quicker out of the blacksmith's shop.

zinnnng *thud*

A crossbow bolt whizzed past Torfulson and stuck into the bellows' wooden frame only inches away.

"Push it down the hill, then get on!" frantically commanded Menderchuck.

The blacksmith reached into his pocket and hurriedly pulled out a new crossbow bolt. For a moment, he fumbled with it, then recovered and reloaded his crossbow. He lifted the crossbow to his eye just in time to see the giant bellows reach the crest of the King's Highway, then disappear out of sight.

Torfulson scrambled on top of the giant wheeled bellows while Menderchuck leapt onto its side. Under the force of gravity, the bellows began to roll downhill, gaining worrisome speed.

"So far, so good," declared a rumbling Menderchuck.

The bellows' mighty frame creaked and shook wildly, bouncing and rolling down the King's Highway at break neck speed.

"Good?! What do we do now?" asked a scared Torfulson.

"I don't know, it was your plan."

With a face full of fear, Torfulson looked back at Menderchuck and shrugged.

"Alright," replied Menderchuck. "I'll figure something out."

Torfulson clung desperately to the top of the bellows' massive frame while Menderchuck cautiously began to work his way toward the back of the speeding frame which careened dangerously down the road. As Menderchuck approached the frame's left back wheel, he paused for a moment to catch his breath. The wheel spun in a mighty blur, ready to crush any who dared get in its way.

White knuckled, gripping the frame for dear life, Menderchuck steeled himself, then swung his body over the speeding wheel. His feet twisted and turned over the death wheel, landing firmly on the back of the frame. Though the frame jostled and shook him, Menderchuck clung resolutely to the frame's back, intently scanning the wheel beside him.

"Where is it?! Where is it?!" frantically mumbled Menderchuck to himself. "There it is!"

As the wheel spun dangerously below him, Menderchuck smiled to himself for a moment, then stomped down on the wheel's foot brake.

craAACCKKK

The foot brake splintered in two, flying off behind them while the bellows continued to recklessly zoom down the King's Highway.

"What was that sound?" worriedly shouted Torfulson. "That didn't sound good."

"Everything's fine! It's all fine!" lied Menderchuck.

Menderchuck gulped, looking down at the speeding wheel beside him. In one fluid motion, he lifted up his left foot, then pressed it down with all his might upon the wheel. Suddenly, Torfulson and Menderchuck's bodies jolted to the right, gripping the bellows frame for dear life, as the bellows turned hard left off of the King's Highway, disappearing into a dark alley.

Like a rabid bull in a china shop, the bellows crashed violently into the narrow alley, smashing through a chicken coop. Feathers, eggs, and a few very surprised chickens were sent flying in all directions. Torfulson, still atop the rumbling bellows, ducked in an attempt avoid the debris. *crack* *crack* *crack* Came the sound of several airborne eggs smashing into Torfulson's head, yolk dripping down his startled face.

Yet despite the coop collision, the bellows continued hurtling dangerously forward through the cramped alleyway.

"Uhhh... uhhhh," grunted Menderchuck, desperately holding onto to the back of the bellows' frame, frantically searching for a solution to their precarious predicament.

Menderchuck's eyes glanced back and forth between the frame's two speeding back wheels. Cautiously, he inched himself into the frame's center back, then he spread his legs as far apart as he could, placing one foot on each back wheel.

"Please work," mumbled Menderchuck under his breath.

The bellows crashed through a clothesline, ripping the lines from the alley walls, taking several sheets and dresses with it. As Torfulson wiped the yolk from his eye, his head was rudely caught by the clothesline. In the blink of an eye, Torfulson's body spun backwards off of the speeding frame and landed with a hard thud upon the dirt alley. Menderchuck grimaced, watching his son's body fly overhead.

"UGGGHH," groaned Menderchuck, putting the full weight of his body upon the two back wheels.

The leather on the bottom of Menderchuck's boots dug into wheels as the wheels fought back trying to resist them. With the entire weight of the barbarian's body behind them, the boots began to get the upper hand. Slowly, the giant bellows began to lose speed, eventually coming to a stop. No sooner had the bellows stopped, then Menderchuck leapt from the cart, throwing off his boots.

"Owww, owww, owww! Hot!" he yelled.

Torfulson, still laying on the ground, looked down the alley at the bellows and its swath of destruction. Then he heard a commotion from behind him. He turned back and saw the blacksmith and several guards running down the King's Highway past the entrance to the dark alley. In an instant, Torfulson popped up to his feet and ran over to Menderchuck, who stood there nursing his own feet.

"They didn't see us come down here. What do we do?" anxiously inquired Torfulson.

"Well, maybe, oh my..."

"What, what is it?" demanded Torfulson.

For a moment, Menderchuck stared at the wide thin clothesline shaped welt that prominently ran across Torfulson's forehead.

"Nothing, it's nothing, you look fine," stumbled Menderchuck.

"Okayyyy?... But what do we do?!"

Menderchuck thought for a second, then walked over to the front of the giant bellows. The clothes line, some peasant clothes, and a sheet were still draped off of it. He pulled the sheet from the clothes line and covered the bellows with it. Then he used the clothes line to tie the sheet tight around the bellows' frame, turning to Torfulson with a self satisfied grin.

"Yeah, yeah, that might work," hastily agreed Torfulson. "But we'll have to take it out through a side gate. They'll be looking along the King's Highway. And we have to do it now. I have to get this attached to the milking contraption as soon as possible. It won't be long before word gets out about this."

Menderchuck just nodded, trying not to stare at the massive welt upon Torfulson's head. Then the two men began to slowly push the bellows down the dark alleyway.

CHAPTER 30:
BUILDING THE CONTRAPTION

The morning cock crowed as the first rays of dawn began to wash over the green countryside around Jennix's dairy farm.

"Shut up you dumb bird!" screamed out farmer Jennix, still laying in bed in the nearby farmhouse.

The rooster took little notice of Jennix's screaming. It was his duty to greet the morning sun, and, by the gods, no one would stop him from his duty. Proudly, the rooster fluttered his wings, then stretched his neck back for all to hear his morning greeting.

"URRRR-UR-URRR-UR-URRR"
THWACK

A boot flew from the farmhouse window, arched across the garden, then smashed into the rooster's head. Cold cocked, the rooster fell silently, limply to the ground.

"I just need five more minutes...." grumbled Jennix to himself, rolling over in bed.

While farmer Jennix drifted back to sleep, and the farm's ranch hands began to slowly rub the sleep from their eyes; there was one man who had already been up for hours. All alone, on a small stool beneath the roof of the farm's great open air milking barn, sat Torfulson, hard at work.

Hours earlier, when the dark of night still ruled the sky, Torfulson and Menderchuck had covertly wheeled the blacksmith's great bellows into the barn. Once the great frame had been rolled into place, Torfulson had cut free the sheet which covered it. Revealed before them was not only the mighty bellows upon its massive wheeled frame, but also, resting upon the great wooden frame, a host of wooden planks, cogs, levers, and gears; all painstaking handcrafted by the two men, according to Torfulson's exacting specifications over the last months.

Quietly, the two men began to lift the parts from the bellows' great frame and spread them out carefully along the ground.

"Make a pile of the small gears over here," Torfulson had commanded. "And make a pile of the pins and support planks there, that'll make it easier to find the parts as we need them."

While Menderchuck sorted the parts, Torfulson began to assemble the milking contraption under the flicker of lamplight. For hours, the two men toiled. Menderchuck helped as he could, holding the light, passing parts to Torfulson, lifting the planks upright so that they could be joined.

As the last stars of night twinkled high above, the two men in the vast milking barn stepped back to admire their work. Before them was Torfulson's great milking contraption. It stood several heads taller than either man. Built onto the bellow's great wooden frame, was a even bigger frame full of interconnected gears, dials, pulleys, and levers, all connected to the great bellows.

"I still have to connect the milking hoses, tighten a few gears, and make some final adjustments," announced Torfulson. "But I can do that on my own. Feel free to go home and get some sleep."

A very tired Menderchuck said not a word. He just put a reassuring hand on Torfulson's shoulder, then turned and began to walk out of the barn.

"Oh," began Torfulson. "One more thing."

Menderchuck stopped in his tracks and looked back at his son who stood beside the immense milking contraption.

"Thank you father, for everything."

Silently, Menderchuck nodded in response, then turned again and exited the barn.

That had been over an hour ago. The final adjustments had taken much longer than Torfulson had anticipated.

"URRRR-UR-URRR-UR-URRR" *THWACK*

Came the sounds of the rooster crowing from the garden.

"Come on. Come on. I'm running out of time!" exclaimed Torfulson, sweat dripping off of his brow as he attempted to attach the last milking hose to the contraption. "Hook up, you blasted thing!"

Like a intrepid explorer fighting an anaconda, Torfulson wrestled against the main hose until he finally managed to slide it onto the bellows' nozzle. Quickly, he placed a clamp around the hose, locking it tightly in place. Then he let out a tired sigh and leaned against the finished milking contraption. For the first time in hours, his focus changed from the contraption before him to the farm around him.

There, one hundred yards away, under the light of the morning sun, was Dale the ranch hand. Calmly, he stood beside the open doors of one of the farm's wide cattle barns.

"No, no, no!" gasped a wild eyed Torfulson, breaking into a sprint across the farmyard towards the cattle barn. "Don't let Mrs. O'Leary out, I need her!"

Torfulson watched in abject panic, watching cow after cow exit the barn and pass by Dale on their way to the south pasture. Torfulson redouble his speed, panting and gasping for air, flying across the farmyard. For a brief moment, he stumbled upon a small rock before regaining his balance and continuing forward. Doggedly, he pushed his body onward, though it screamed for him to stop. As he finally approached the cattle barn, he came to a skidding stop just feet away from Dale.

"Iff m'ldy dare?" spouted out a breathless Torfulson.

"What?" asked a confused Dale. "Does your lady dare to do what? Is this a saucy riddle, cause you know I'm not good at those."

Torfulson shook his head while a stitch of pain ran through his side.

"Isss m'olry stilin barn?" exhaled Torfulson through labored breathes.

"Who in the world in Mollery? Some new milkmaid? Is she cute? Maybe you should catch your breath a second, Torfulson."

Torfulson tried for a third time, "Mrs. O'Leary, is she still in the barn?"

"Why? Jennix want you to get an early start on milking her?"

"Sureee.. YES, he definitely said that!" lied Torfulson.

"Sorry, she's already long gone to the south pasture."

"Nooooo," cried out Torfulson, stumbling backwards.

"Ha, ha, ha, look at your face," laughed out Dale. "Oh that's priceless. No worries though, I was just messing with you. She's still in the barn, back left stall, the big one."

Torfulson's anger at having been deceived was instantly washed away by an immense feeling of relief. Hastily, he darted past the out going cows on his way into the barn. He rushed to the back left stall, the big one. There, as Dale had prophesied, he found the farm's prized dairy cow, Mrs. O'Leary.

CHAPTER 31:
THE MILKING CONTRAPTION

"Hurry!" ordered Torfulson, leading Mrs. O'Leary out of her stall.

Torfulson pulled on the cow, and he pushed on the cow with all his might, trying to rush the creature from the cattle barn to the milking barn, but she was having none of it. Impatiently, he watched the rest of the herd leave the cattle barn on their way towards the south pasture while Mrs. O'Leary slowly plodded along. She was determined to have a leisurely stroll to the milking barn and so she did.

By the time Torfulson and Mrs. O'Leary finally reached the edge of the milking barn, Jennix's farm had begun to rustle with the sounds of ranch hands and milkmaids getting ready for work. Torfulson led the cow beneath the milking barn's great roof toward the milking contraption. It was then that Mrs. O'Leary stopped suddenly. The cow eyed the large milking machine warily, refusing to approach it.

"Come on girl," gently encouraged Torfulson. "We need to get you closer for this to work."

Torfulson pushed on Mrs. O'Leary's side in attempt to guide her towards the machine, but Mrs. O'Leary pushed back, sending Torfulson tumbling awkwardly to the ground. A smattering of chuckles sprung up around him. Torfulson looked up from the ground to see a small group of milkmaids and ranch hands (including Dale) watching him.

"Yeah, my Misses gets ornery like that too, when I try and push her around," laughed Dale, before biting off the tip of a carrot that he was holding.

Torfulson sprung to his feet, rushed over to Dale, and snatched the carrot from his hand.

"Hey! I was eating that!" impotently protested Dale.

Carrot in hand, Torfulson slowly approached the prized dairy cow. He placed a reassuring hand upon her neck and then began to whisper in her ear.

"Look, I, I, I get your nervous. Honestly, I am too. Tell you what," bargained Torfulson. "You help me out with this, and I'll personally get you a lifetime supply of carrots."

Torfulson patted the cow's neck with one hand while his other hand held the carrot just out of reach in front of the cow. Mrs. O'Leary stepped towards the carrot. With each step, Torfulson moved the carrot, guiding the cow towards the immense milking machine. Once Mrs. O'Leary was in place besides the machine, Torfulson reward her with the carrot, then quickly set to work.

The milking contraption's main hose snaked from the giant bellows' nozzle to a great glass jug. Four smaller hoses emerged from the glass jug, their unattached ends laying on the barn's dirt floor. Carefully, one by one, Torfulson began to attach the smaller hoses to Mrs. O'Leary's teats.

"What's that?" asked Dale.

"My ticket," answered a distracted Torfulson.

"Don't look like no ticket I've ever seen."

"It's my ticket to a better life," explained Torfulson. "Goodbye poverty, hello new shoes. It's a milking contraption. It's going to revolutionize the industry."

The words "milking contraption" set off a small buzz of chuckles and chatter amongst the group of ranch hands and milkmaids who were now intently watching Torfulson's progress. Most had seen or heard the story of Torfulson's last "milking contraption," and didn't want to miss out on this newest opportunity to see him fail spectacularly.

Torfulson took little notice of the growing crowd. He gently tugged on the last of the four small hoses, which were connected to Mrs. O'Leary's teats, to make sure that it was secure. Then he stood up and walked over to the side of the immense milking contraption.

"Carry, the one. Seventeen, no, no sixteen..." mumbled Torfulson, grabbing the hair on the side of his head. "That should be sufficient torque, as long as the flywheel holds..."

Torfulson made one final adjustment to the machine, then stepped back to take it all in.

"I can't believe it," proudly smiled Torfulson. "It's a thousand times better than my first design. Months of work, almost all of my money, but it's done. It's finally done."

The blacksmith's giant bellows, transformed into a massive milking contraption, dominated the barn's interior. Beside the great machine, Mrs. O'Learly calmly stood, eating her carrot, while a host of curious ranch hands and milkmaids watched on in eager anticipation of what was to come.

"Let's make history," whispered Torfulson with a bit of trepidation, stepping up to the contraption and pulling one of its levers.

Then he firmly grasped the crank, which stuck out of the machine's side, and began to turn it slowly and methodically. As the crank turned, so too did the multitude of gears in the machine. They clacked softly in rotation, one gear turning the next, and then the next. The great flywheel, near the top of the machine, began to slowly rotate, pushing a rod up and down. With each push of the rod, the great bellows began to slowly rise, filling with air.

While the crowd watched the clattering clacking machine in awe, Torfulson's eyes remained transfixed upon the glass jug. Desperately, he looked for even the smallest drop of milk, but saw none.

"Looks like it works about as well as Bill's wife," teased Dale to a smattering of laughter from the crowd.

Needless to say, the nearby ranch hand Bill was not amused.

"Come on, come on," grunted Torfulson, trying to will the machine into producing milk.

Torfulson furrowed his brow and crossed his arms, staring at the machine for a moment. Then he hastily grabbed a lever and adjusted its position. Next he grabbed the crank on the side of the machine and spun it harder. The clatter of the machine's gears and flywheel began to grow, spinning faster.

Once again, Torfulson gazed down at the glass jug beside farmer Jennix's prize cow in hope of seeing some drops of milk. And once again, he disappointingly saw nothing.

"Ugghhh," frustratedly groaned Torfulson.

"Torfulson!" screamed out an angry voice from behind him.

Surprised, Torfulson and the crowd spun around to see farmer Jennix standing there with fury upon his face.

"What in the hells are you doing to my cow?!"

"Sir, I'm..." Torfulson tried to explain.

"Shut up!" commanded Jennix, stomping over to Torfulson with his eyes fixated upon the hoses that were connected to his prized cow. "Not another milking contraption. I said no! Get that off of Mrs. O'Leary before you hurt her, ya idiot!"

Farmer Jennix's face flushed red with rage. Torfulson was no stranger to Jennix's anger. In the many years that he had worked for Jennix, Torfulson had become quite adept at bowing his head and just saying "yes sir." But at that moment, something changed inside of him.

Defiantly, Torfulson slammed a lever into an upright position, then turned the crank as fast as he could. The machine began to vibrate and whine louder and louder while its gears turned faster and faster. The machine's rotating flywheel became a spinning blur. The giant bellows let out audible gasps as the rods that drove it attempted to suck in more and more air.

"I said to..!" continued the furious farmer Jennix.

"Shut up, you old coot!" shouted Torfulson. "This machine is going to make you and me, and, and, and the blacksmith rich! In one day it'll be able to do the work of a hundred milkmaids. If you weren't so ding dong pig headed, you'd have the patience to see that!"

Torfulson pointed towards the glass jug beneath the cow and held his breath. It was this, or nothing. Farmer Jennix, the assembled crowd of milkmaids and ranch hands, and Torfulson stared at the jug with hushed anticipation. And then it finally happened.

First there was a tiny split, and then there was a tiny splat. A drop of milk, pulled through the hoses, dropped into the bottom of the glass jug, and then another, and then another. The clattering of the contraption filled the silent barn while the milking machine began to draw steady milk streams out of the cow's udder in quick even strokes. Milk quickly begun to rise in the glass jug.

Gobsmacked, Jennix turned towards Torfulson, "Did ya say something about money?"

"Yes!" replied Torfulson, clapping in joy. "With these milking contraptions you can increase the herd a hundred fold, and only have to pay for all the employees you currently have. You can even give them raises."

"Lets not get too hasty about raises..." mumbled farmer Jennix. "Really, one hundred fold?"

Triumphantly, Torfulson folded his arms and nodded. Jennix paused for a moment, watching the milking machine work before him, then a great smile erupted upon his face. To the crowd's great surprise, Jennix placed a friendly arm around Torfulson's shoulder.

"Torfulson! You're a genius! I always believed in you, that's why I kept ya on all these years."

The glass jug filled with more and more milk while Mrs. O'Leary stood there peacefully.

"I want to buy this contraption!" declared farmer Jennix, who was now a very enthusiastic convert to the cause. "Or maybe, better yet, you should just become my partner. We're going to be rich! No one else has one of these. Imagine the possibilities!"

"Well," timidly admitted Torfulson. "We have to include the blacksmith in the partnership, as his bellows are a part of the machine."

"Sure, sure, we'll make him a junior partner or something."

"MooooOOOO," lowed Mr's. O'Leary, who seemed to have a slightly pained expression upon her long face.

The cluttering and clacking of the contraption grew, its gears spinning faster and faster. The bellows huffed and puffed under the pressure, drawing more and more milk out of the cow at an ever increasing rate.

"Ummm, I think I need to slow the contraption a bit..." worried Torfulson aloud.

"Nonsense, son," replied Jennix. "We're talking business here, that can wait."

"MooooOOO!!!!" exclaimed the cow again, definitely in pain.

Hurriedly, Torfulson reached for the machine, pressing in a lever. The machine began to tremble and rock, moving faster and faster. Frantically, he tried pulling and pushing other levers to slow the speeding machine to no avail.

"Slow down... Slow down..." anxiously mumbled Torfulson.

Desperately, he grabbed the crank on the side of the machine and tried to spin it backwards. To his dismay, he heard the sounds of stripping of gears. Small gears poured out from the machine as the crank fell off in his hand.

The spinning flywheel atop the machine began to wobble precariously, emitting a high pitched whine. The great rods that pushed the bellows continued to accelerate. With each stroke, the giant bellows let out a mighty wheezing sound, sucking harder and harder upon the hoses.

"Never mind that, Torfulson," scoffed Jennix, waving a dismissively greedy hand. "That's no big problem. We can fix that. Why don't we just sign a partnership contract right now, as fast as we can?"

But the thing is, there was a problem, a big problem. Torfulson, the ranch hands, and the milkmaids watched the milking contraption rock wildly in helpless anxiety. The whine of the rapidly rotating flywheel grew louder and louder. The giant bellows wheezed with a deep and unsettling bass note. In one last desperate move, Torfulson grabbed two of the machine's levers at once and pulled back on them with all of his might. To his horror, they broke off in his hands.

"MOOOOOOO!!!" screeched out Mr's O'Leary the cow.

A great many life altering things would happen in the next short seconds. The immense sucking power of the contraption tried to pull the entire cow into the glass jug all at once. Needless to say, a one ton prized cow can not fit comfortably inside of a five gallon glass jug. In an instant, a bloody hamburger like substance was pulled into the glass jug until it could hold it no longer. Then the entire cow and jug exploded loudly in a shower of frothy milk, broken glass, and large chunks of bloody beef which violently careened throughout the barn. Instantly, a great many ranch hands and milkmaids were flattened by flying chunks of beef which rudely knocked them from their feet and onto the ground.

The center of the barn looked as though a bomb had gone off. Though all would survive, a great many would have deep beef inflicted trauma for years to come. It was said afterwards that pieces of cow were even found in fields miles way.

Stunned, Torfulson and Jennix stood silently next to each other in the aftermath of the cowsplosion. Each drenched in cow blood and covered in cow parts. It was like wearing a whole butcher's shop on oneself. That is, if the butcher had chopped up an entire cow directly above you. A two inch chunk of the glass jar stood partially embedded in farmer Jennix's left bicep. Shakily, Torfulson wiped bits of blood and cow from his face. Weakly, he turned towards Jennix.

"So... about that partnership..."

"PARTNERSHIP?!" furiously screamed out farmer Jennix, pulling the glass shard from his arm. "You moron! You killed Mr's O'Leary, and you almost killed me!"

"But..." Torfulson tried to reason. "You said it

wasn't a big problem..."

Farmer Jennix's face was covered in cow blood. His eyes glared maniacally, staring at Torfulson.

"You're right Torfulson," menacingly agreed Jennix. "There's only one problem we need to figure out."

"What's that...?"

Farmer Jennix ran over to a nearby support beam and pulled off a hanging metal pitchfork.

"How I'm going to kill you!" shouted Jennix.

Pitchfork in hand, farmer Jennix began to violently charge towards Torfulson. As he quickly lurched across the barn, Jennix stepped into a puddle of what had been cow just moments before. His feet scrambled desperately below him trying to gain traction, but to no avail. His arms flailed about wildly as he crashed into the barn's gore covered dirt floor.

"This is my moment to do something brave," thought Torfulson to himself.

And thus, Torfulson turned his back to the angry farmer and ran away, as fast as his feet would carry him.

CHAPTER 32: RUN

Torfulson's speeding feet kicked up small clouds of dirt and gravel as he ran full tilt down the King's Highway towards Oppidium. Some might have said that he was trying to outrun the embarrassment of his failed milking contraption. He would have said that he was trying to outrun the vengeful wrath of farmer Jennix. Either way, months of planning, hard work, and all of his life savings were now destroyed in the bloody cow explosion.

The sun shone down upon the lush green landscape which surrounded the dirt road. Nearby, birds playfully hopped and sang, but all that Torfulson heard was the pounding of his heart in his ears. As Torfulson approached a fork in the road, he began to slow. Wheezing, he doubled over in pain, sides stinging, desperately gasping for air.

An old rickety hay cart, driven by an old rickety man, slowly passed through the fork in the road on its way to Oppidium. Paranoid, Torfulson looked back over his shoulder along the road he had just traveled. There, behind him, he saw a rapidly advancing cloud of dust.

"Jennix!" gasped Torfulson between pained breaths.

Fear raced through Torfulson's eyes while they desperately sought for options. It was then that his eyes locked onto the rickety old cart. With his last ounce of strength, he ran forward and leapt into the back of the cart. Then he burrowed deep beneath the pile of hay that it carried, praying it would be a sufficient hiding place. In very short order, he heard the sound of racing hooves.

"Please pass by, please pass by," frantically whispered Torfulson to himself.

But the sounds of a multitude of racing hooves did not pass by. They slowed to a stop besides the rickety old cart.

"Old man!" exclaimed a voice.

Torfulson's blood went cold. It was certainly the voice of the farmer Jennix, who was leading a posse of armed ranch hands.

"What do you all want?" asked the curmudgeonly old man, pulling his small horse drawn cart to a stop.

"Have you seen a lanky good for nothing peasant running down this road?" demanded an angry Jennix.

Fear gripped Torfulson, shaking him like a hurricane. It screamed at him to flee, but he refused to listen. Instead, he lay perfectly still in the bottom of the wagon.

"Hmmm," thought the old man aloud. "My memory isn't what it used to be. Perhaps it could be jogged with a bit of coin."

"Ugh," grunted Jennix, reaching into his pockets and retrieving a gold coin.

Reluctantly, he placed it into the old man's greedy outstretched hand. A large smile spread across the old man's face as he lifted up the gold coin, watching it glint in the sunlight.

"Well, did you see him?!" demanded an impatient Jennix.

"No, I didn't see anything," replied the grinning old man.

Furious, Jennix pulled his horse up close to the cart, then punched the old man in the face. As fist collided with elderly face, the old man fell awkwardly off of the cart, hitting the hard ground with a loud fart.

"Ohhh, my wife warned me this would happen," painfully groaned the old man.

"Search the hay!" commanded Jennix.

Obediently, several of the ranch hands dismounted, pulled short swords from their scabbards, and walked menacingly over to the side of the hay cart.

"Please don't kill me," silently prayed Torfulson, closing his eyes and preparing for the worst.

THUD *THUD* *THUD* The points of the blades stabbed wildly into the hay pile, raining down around Torfulson, colliding with the wagon's hard bed. One landed just a hair's breadth away from his ear, but Torfulson remained perfectly still.

"There's nothing here boss," yelled out Dale the ranch hand.

"Mount up boys!" commanded Jennix, eyes glaring, nostrils flaring. "We're heading to the city. Maybe we can find that good for nothing Torfulson there!"

From deep under the hay pile, Torfulson heard the sounds of hooves charging off. Only then did his guard drop, letting out a huge sigh of relief.

With a groan, the rickety old man pushed himself to his feet, then climbed back up onto the rickety old cart.

"Well Maybelle," confided the old man to the horse who pulled the cart. "I think I dun soiled me self. That's a bit embarrassing, I must say. Well, let's just keep that between us."

"I won't tell a soul," came Torfulson's hidden voice floating out of the hay.

"Who said that?!" gasped the old man.

The old man rapidly spun his body around, but saw no one there. His head frantically twisted around in search of the voice, but his eyes only saw the hay cart and the singing birds of the nearby fields. Slowly, he turned his head towards his horse, staring at it with a quizzical look on his face.

"Did you say that Maybelle?" whispered the unsure old man.

The horse said not a word.

"Maybe I should have named you Roger, or Fred," mumbled the very confused old man.

The old man lifted the horse's reigns in his hands and gave them a light flick. With a creak, the hay cart began to slowly roll towards Oppidium once again.

CHAPTER 33: END OF THE LINE

A lone man rushed through the back alleyways of Oppidium's slums. He flew past some young peasant children making mud pies in the street. He ran by a dilapidated horse cart carrying trash. He sped past the ramshackled houses that lined the street.

"Home... gotta get home, then figure out what to do," frantically mumbled Torfulson.

He turned a corner and bull rushed down the final dark alleyway. His destination was almost in sight. No sooner had his right foot left the dark alley, stepping into the sunlit street beyond, when he was leapt on from behind.

"Mmmrpphh!" gasped Torfulson, his startled scream muffled by the mysterious hand that now forcefully covered his mouth.

Gripping him from behind, pinning his arms back, the unknown assailant dragged Torfulson back into the alley's dark shadows against his will. For a moment, Torfulson lashed and flailed about, struggling desperately against the strong arms that restrained him, but to no avail. Then the assailant slowly removed his hand from Torfulson's mouth.

"Don't kill me!" pleaded Torfulson, trying to look behind him.

"Don't try to shave me again, and we'll be good," smiled Menderchuck, who wore his weapons upon his body.

Torfulson stumbled forward as Menderchuck released him from his grip.

"You ass! Why'd you jump me...."

Menderchuck held up a lone finger to his lips for silence, then pointed diagonally across the sunlit street towards Torfulson's rustic home. A half dozen heavily armed guards patrolled around the shack. The shack's front door lay upon the ground, brutally smashed to pieces.

"Noooo..." cried Torfulson, watching intently as the blacksmith stepped out of the shack and walked over to one of the guards.

Menderchuck grabbed Torfulson's arm, gently pulling him further back into the shadows of the narrow alleyway.

"They're looking for you for stealing the bellows," explained Menderchuck in hushed tones.

"Oh gods," lamented Torfulson. "Wait.... don't you mean looking for us?"

"Nope, I just went up and talked to them," answered Menderchuck. "They didn't recognize me at all, but... that's not the case for you. Apparently your stupid mask came off in the robbery, and the blacksmith got a good look at your face. They've got your mask, if you want it back."

"They didn't see you at all?"

"Nope, I'm like a cat in the dark," meowed Menderchuck, pantomiming a cat.

Torfulson glared with annoyance, "Like that so called alarm cat you kicked, giving us away!"

"I stand by what I did. I'd do it again," resolutely replied Menderchuck.

Torfulson let out a deep mournful sigh, watching the city guards who now surrounded his home.

"Sooo..." eagerly ventured Menderchuck. "How about the milking contraption? Did it work? Of course it must have, you're a smart kid. Can we go tell them that everything is good now?"

Crestfallen, Torfulson shook his head no.

"My life is ruined... ruined," the melancholy words poured from Torfulson's mouth. "Those bellows were worth more than me. It should have worked... it did work.... kinda. What am I going to do?"

A quiet silence filled the dark alley while Menderchuck tried to find some comforting words.

"Well..." suggested Menderchuck. "If you've given up on the contraption, we could always return the bellows and apologize. I'm charismatic, maybe I can talk them down to a fine or something."

Torfulson shook his head again, "They're gone forever. All that's left is tiny bits of wood, leather, and cow."

"Oh...."

"I'm done," lamented Torfulson. "My life is over."

"If you're alive, then there's always options, even if you don't like them," declared Menderchuck. "What are your options?"

"Well," ruminated Torfulson. "I guess I have two. Option one, I turn myself in and trust to the mercy of the court."

"Is the court merciful?"

"Not particularly," explained Torfulson. "Just the other week, an old washer woman got sent to twenty years hard labor for accidentally over starching the Lord Mayor's codpiece. If I was lucky, I'd be sentenced to debtor's prison until I could pay off the bellows... and the cow, which would be never. In effect a life sentence, and that's if I'm lucky. People have been hung for less."

"And Option two?" asked Menderchuck.

"I dunno... run away from everything. Leave Oppidium and never come back..."

Menderchuck put a sympathetic hand on Torfulson's shoulder.

"I'm sorry..."

"It's not your fault," interrupted Torfulson. "It was my stupid plan to build a milking contraption."

"Oh no, not that," retorted Menderchuck, carelessly waving away Torfulson's concern. "Last night, you and me, stealing that bellows, well it was amazing! A father and son raiding adventure! I... I don't know what I missed out on by not being there to see you grow up, but, well... I have a feeling that I missed out on a lot, and I now regret it. I'm sorry I wasn't there to see you grow up. You're a bit of a dork, but I wish I'd gotten to know you much earlier in life. Now enough of this crap town. Let's go, the future awaits!"

"But... my home..." sadly sighed Torfulson.

"It's not your home anymore."

Menderchuck turned away from the shack, that he had been living in for the past months, and began to boldly stroll down the dark alleyway. Torfulson took one last longing look at the only home that he had ever known. His shoulders slunk and his head hung low.

"Why does life always have to be so hard?" despondently mumbled Torfulson.

Torfulson looked down to his feet and saw a small stone. He gave the stone a swift kick, sending it rolling down the dirty alley. Then he slowly turned his back to his broken home and followed Menderchuck into the future.

THE
END

Thank you for taking the time to read
"The Barbarian Menderchuck."

If you enjoyed it, please consider sharing it
with a friend or leaving a review.
Have a great day!

You can find our other novels and rpg
adventure modules at:

www.zansadventures.com